ENDORSEMENTS

It has been my pleasure to know Marcia Williams for over fifteen years, evolving from mere acquaintances to partners in ministry. The *Women in Pursuit* initiative was birthed in a living room that transformed into a delivery and recovery space. Since its inception, I have observed her spiritual growth through prayer, evolving into a powerful Prophetic Deliverance Minister of the Gospel. Witnessing her children establish themselves as godly young individuals and entrepreneurs, while appreciating their significant contributions to the Williams legacy, has been truly profound. Her family's impact has transformed the lives of many in Baltimore and its surrounding areas.

Kanita Washington
B'FLY Productions

Unstoppable and undeniable is the woman in pursuit! Visionary author Marcia Williams and her co-authors share that no boundaries can prohibit you from achieving your dreams and entering your destiny. These women are limitless and take the world by force as they achieve victory in every area of their lives. Despite tests, trials, and triumphs, these women discovered that everything they needed was found within themselves. Women in pursuit, *you've got this*!

LaVerne Perlie,
Transform on Purpose, LLC

THE RESILIENCE OF WOMEN IN PURSUIT

MARCIA WILLIAMS

EDITED BY
NICOLE QUEEN

VISION PUBLISHING
HOUSE

ISBN: 978-1-955297-52-3 (Hardback)
ISBN: 978-1-955297-58-5 (Paperback)

LCCN: 2023924174

Vision Publishing House
9103 Woodmore Centre #334
Lanham, MD 20706

www.vision-publishinghouse.com

*This book is dedicated to every woman who weathered her storm, conquered
various obstacles, crossed many bridges, faced failures,
but resiliently rose again!*

*There were moments when you contemplated giving up on yourself, but
somehow you recognized a calling on your life that was greater than you.
Now, you are walking into complete victory and freedom!*

To every woman who is in pursuit of fulfilling her purpose in life...

YOU'VE GOT IT WOMEN!!!

In the past, I didn't know who I was. Now, I admire who I am. But I *really* love who I'm becoming!

— MARCIA WILLIAMS

CONTENTS

Foreword   xi
Introduction   xiii

I AM AWAKENED   I
Markia Cherry

I AM ACCEPTED   9
Monique Debi

I AM AN OVERCOMER   2I
Donique Lomax

I AM RESILIENT   29
Ebony McClenny

I AM FREE   4I
Alicia Smith

I AM CHOSEN   5I
Sherrita Coates

I AM RESTORED   63
Dakiria Jones

I AM A SURVIVOR   69
Terriona Williams

I AM VICTORIOUS   75
Marcia Williams

Words of Encouragement   89
Tributes to Pastor Marcia   9I
Acknowledgments   95
About the Visionary Author   97

FOREWORD

Congratulations are in order to Pastor Marcia Williams for boldly venturing into the exploration of "The Resilience of Women in Pursuit." I've witnessed her elevation from being a minister, to evolving into an elder, and eventually pastoring the people of God at *Abundant Life Purpose Center*, the church she birthed. Throughout her transformation, her fervor for empowering women to pursue and embrace God's power, resilience, and persistence in the face of life's most challenging circumstances has been evident.

I can envision that her life's journey hasn't been a walk in the park; there were likely days when she contemplated throwing in the towel, and faced both personal and ministry crises. This literary work stands as a testament of God's love, faithfulness, goodness, purpose, and destiny in her life. Jeremiah 1:5 expresses it perfectly, "Before I formed thee in the belly, I knew thee, and before thou camest forth out of the womb I sanctified thee, and I ordained thee a prophet unto the nations."

I am confident that women across the country, as they delve into this book, will comprehend their God-given purpose and find the courage to accept that they are extraordinary overcomers. Their faith will be rejuvenated; they will be fortified to embrace resilience and freedom as restored and chosen vessels to the glory of God!

Thank you, Pastor Marcia Williams, for this powerful reminder that we are survivors and victors!

In His Service,

First Lady A. Faye Bell
Greater Paradise Christian Center

INTRODUCTION

This book is a testament to the incredible strength and resilience of women who have triumphed over seemingly insurmountable obstacles, and it underscores the pivotal role that faith in God has played in propelling them forward. These women's journeys are nothing short of remarkable; they have evolved from enduring profound pain and adversity to achieving remarkable personal growth and success. It's like witnessing a beautiful metamorphosis unfold before your eyes. In their darkest moments, they turned to God, allowing His power to manifest in their lives, transforming what seemed like ashes into exquisite beauty. Much like diamonds, these women have been tested and battered by life's challenges, but they have emerged from the crucible of their experiences as radiant beings.

Within the pages of this book, you'll be captivated by the inspiring stories of nine women who have not only survived, but thrived by wholeheartedly embracing their God-given talents, creative gifts, and divine purposes. Their stories transcend the boundaries of different life domains, encompassing endeavors in business, relationships, motherhood, and various aspirations. Their narratives are more than just tales of personal triumph; they are a source of profound inspiration.

Each woman's journey is a testament of resilience, reminding us that we, too, possess the ability to overcome adversities. These stories carry the profound message that, with faith and unwavering determination, we can rise above our challenges and limitations. They encourage us to embrace the fullness of our potential and to have the courage to pursue our dreams, no matter the obstacles in our path.

Drawing from the wisdom of Revelation 12:11, which tells us that victory is achieved through both faith and the testimony of one's experiences, the women within these pages have courageously shattered the limitations that life may have imposed on them. In doing so, they have illuminated a path for others to follow—one that leads to empowerment, transformation, and ultimately, triumph over adversity.

I Am Awakened

MARKIA CHERRY

The Bible says, "For I know the plans I have for you," declares the Lord, "plans to prosper you and not to harm you, plans to give you hope and a future" (Jeremiah 29:11). Well, let's start by saying that I have not always believed this Scripture. I struggled with my identity and purpose. I often questioned why I existed in the first place. I often felt like I didn't quite fit in, and I was a bit of a loner, despite being somewhat popular.

Growing up as a young black girl in an area where some people considered the projects was no easy feat. My mother, a single parent raising three girls, was battling a drug addiction during that time. But let me be clear, my mom is truly remarkable. Back then, I didn't even realize we were living in poverty; it just felt like our norm.

She did whatever it took to provide for us, and I couldn't tell that we were struggling, financially. However, there were times when we had no electricity and sometimes no food. This pushed me into taking on adult responsibilities at a very young age, and survival skills became second nature to me. I started paying bills when I was just thirteen years old. I lied on my job application to start working early because, to be honest, I looked older than my age, so I took the risk.

My main motivation was to assist my mom, who, at this point, had turned her life around and chosen her children over her past drug abuse. I have to say, it was one of the happiest days when she came to visit the church I was attending, thanks to my pre-kindergarten teacher who brought me there when I was only six years old (that's a story in itself). I would hand over my entire paychecks to her, and sometimes I even resorted to stealing from my job to help pay the bills.

She never asked where I got the money from, which I'm grateful for because I never wanted to lie to her. She was my hero, and all I wanted was to make her happy and proud of me. She loved each and every one of my siblings and did the best she could, despite being a young mother, herself. While this journey was far from easy, it taught me valuable life lessons: how to survive, be responsible, stay diligent, stay ambitious, provide for others, never give up, be a giver, and always prioritize family.

Although I learned a lot of principles at such a young age, I always felt that I was missing something. As a child, I longed for the love of my biological father. Without realizing it at the time, I sought traces of him in the men I dated. I remember being a child and him telling me, "Boo-boo, I'll be home for your high school graduation." I waited anxiously with anticipation. My high school graduation came and went, and the same happened with my undergraduate and graduate university graduations. He didn't attend either one.

My dad served ten years in prison, but unfortunately, he ended up back there for another ten years. I tried my best to bury the emptiness I felt deep inside and focused on my accomplishments in life, while desperately seeking love. My once anxious attachment style evolved into an avoidant attachment style. To escape the pain of my dad's absence, I completely avoided thinking about it; I pushed it to the back of my mind. I thought that if I ignored it, I would never have to deal with it. Little did I know that I would see traces of my dad in every man I chose to date. Without proper healing, therapy, or counseling, I ended up repeating the same patterns.

I started dating, and I went through a series of relationships with men. Each relationship taught me something valuable about myself. My last two relationships ended in a whirlwind. They were two men whom I loved dearly, but in very different ways. The way they were ripped out of my life was like déjà vu. Both were murdered by gun violence and betrayal.

I was mad at God for a while. Trauma, hurt, bitterness, anger, and paranoia became second nature to me. I often wonder why God would take away something so pure, genuine, and real. In my last relationship, I believed I had found everything I desired in a man — a great personality, ambition, good looks, security, and personal growth. It felt like the long wait for the perfect partner was finally over. Did I mention he was incredibly *fiiiiiiine!* He treated me like the queen I am, seeing qualities in me that I hadn't recognized in myself, and motivated me in ways I didn't know were possible. He was a true king, and it felt like something out of a fairy tale. I had never experienced such deep love before, to the point where I almost idolized it.

Meanwhile, God had been yearning for my attention. See, I was so busy wrapped up in love that I forgot about God for a season of my life. I've been a runner all my life, running from God's calling, and I became comfortable with my life full of love. I thought I had all I ever wanted, so God had to get my attention— and boy, did He get it! I will never forget that call I received one evening when I was preparing one of our favorite meals that I thought we would share together. On the other line was someone telling me he was gone. *Huh?* I was so confused and so heartbroken. I screamed! My heart jumped completely out of my body, and my mind scrambled. I was screaming to myself, "No, not again!" I was in disbelief.

In a previous relationship, I received a devastating call that my boyfriend had been murdered. Despite being two hours away, I drove frantically to the scene, only to discover that he had passed away instantly. Nearly three years later, I got that same heart-wrenching call again, but this time, I was just eight minutes away from my current boyfriend. I had this irrational hope that if I could touch him, hold him, and make him hear me, he might come back to life. I didn't make it in time for the first tragic incident, but this time, I thought, maybe I could somehow prevent it. I desperately believed, "No, this cannot happen again!"

I began to pray, scream, and weep all at the same time. I rushed to the scene, desperate to reach my boyfriend, but the police stopped me from crossing the caution tape. In my distress, I tried to get to him and ended up in handcuffs. The police were ruthless, showing no empathy. To them, I was just another black woman from the ghetto whose man had been murdered. They didn't offer condolences; in fact, they laughed. When I asked which hospital he was being taken to, their response was dismissive.

Being placed in a paddy wagon was a nightmare for someone with claustrophobia. I screamed in anxiety, begging not to be put in there. My mom and stepdad joined in, pleading for the officers to at least place me in a police car with windows so I could breathe properly. One officer seemed sympathetic, questioning whether they should be locking me up given my recent loss. However, the sergeant decided to proceed with my arrest. They accused me of assaulting an officer, while six officers were trying to pull me away from the caution tape.

Instead of being able to grieve, I spent that night in jail. I was locked up, while the man I believed would be my future husband— the love of my life, my heart outside of my chest— laid lifeless on the cold pavement for over three hours.

During that night in my cell, my mind felt like it was spiraling out of control. My anxiety reached an all-time high. I kept asking myself, "How could this even happen? Why am I even here? What the h%ll is going on? God, how could you let this happen?" It felt like I was having some sort of out-of-body experience, desperately searching for answers about the why, how, who, and when.

As I sat there in that cell, trying to regain some semblance of control, I remembered something my sister had told me years ago. Based on a situation she experienced, she stated that if you seemed to be losing control or screamed while in your cell, the jail authorities might confine you to an empty room and use restraints. So, I did everything I could to maintain my composure. I counted to a million — twice— to gather my thoughts. It was a cold November 3rd night, the same day I had gone to vote in the U.S. Presidential Election. It was a day I would never forget. In that small cell, I felt lifeless, emotionally shattered, abandoned, helpless, and utterly hopeless.

Something in me died that night. For the first time in my life, I realized that no one— not my mother, father, man, sisters, or brothers — could save me. My only refuge in that exact moment was God Himself, God alone. I knew that His grace was sufficient, and His strength was most evident in my weakness. With the little faith I had, as small as a mustard seed, I believed I would be free.

The next morning, as I was getting ready to change into my jump-suit to join the general population from the holding cell, I was released on my own recognizance after seeing the commissioner for the second time. I returned to my luxury condo, once filled with love, now an empty home. There was the meal I had prepared the night before for my man and me— garlic parmesan shrimp with perfectly cooked ground turkey, accompanied by red, green, and orange peppers, along with garlic bread— one of his favorite dishes. I wept, as I threw it all away, not realizing that afternoon would be the last time I would see him. That morning was the last time we made love and worked out in our condo's gym. It was the last time I heard his parting words: "I love you. Take care of A'zumi," our Pomeranian puppy he had bought for me just four months before he was murdered. My man was gone; he was gone forever.

Nothing at that moment surprised me anymore. I became numb. I grew to understand that God permits certain events in your life to get your attention and make you fully reliant on Him. I could no longer run from God's calling on my life. It was only when I started to accept my reality and embark on a journey towards self-love and healing that I discovered my genuine purpose. It had been there all along, but I had been ignoring all the signs. To uncover the rest of my story, stay tuned for my upcoming book series!

*"Awaken! The wait and running aimlessly is over.
Purpose has found me. He has not forgotten me!"*

* * *

My Word of Wisdom to You:

Yes, we go through trials. Trust me, I've had very dark seasons in my life. What I realized, however, is that affliction will leave you with a desire to really connect with the Lord because He knows you cannot go through this battle with your own strength. When He allows us to go through tough times and certain battles, He is refining, molding, shaping, and building true character in us to carry out His divine plan. This situation will build your character and your faith. This set of circumstances will lead you to pray more often and with more urgency. So, be encouraged. He is in control.

He is ever faithful to rescue us all. He is forever faithful. Through my affliction, I realized I needed the Lord even more. Despite what we have gone through, we still have a lot to be thankful for. Trust and believe that the trials God allows us to face will reveal the treasure inside of us. Believe that the trials in your life will uncover the gifts that God has placed inside of you. Accept that we will experience affliction, even as a Child of God. Believe that the affliction will produce a new level of faith in you.

When you have God on your side and His favor upon your life, He will give you victory in every aspect of your life, regardless of how unqualified or unskilled you may think you are. With God, it all works out to your advantage and will work out for your good. Believe that God will reveal the treasure in you. It is all part of His divine plan.

Stay encouraged, as you continue your journey called life. Always remember, that God loves you and that you were thought of before you were in your mother's womb. The Bible says:

"Before I formed you in the womb, I knew you; before you were born, I sanctified you."

— JEREMIAH 1:5

He has a great need for you. Trust in God's plans for your life. His divine plan for you will be unveiled in His perfect timing, and you, too, will be awakened.

You are a woman in pursuit.

I AM ACCEPTED
MONIQUE DEBI

"**B**ut are you gay?" I yelled. My heart was racing. The tightness in the pit of my stomach was consuming me as my body trembled, and I stared into the eyes of my husband of two months. "Answer me, d@mmit!" I yelled.

"Monique— come on— you know me! I ain't gay at all."

It took everything in me not to put my hands on him. All I could do was cry and shake. "Lorenzo, I saw the messages. You were talking to a man about sex! You told him not to take his hormone pills. You wanted him rock-hard when you came over there. You even talked about all of the semen last time you both climaxed!"

Lorenzo stared me in my eyes and didn't utter another word. I was stuck, sitting on the edge of our marriage bed, with his phone in my hands. Our life together was over.

It was confirmed. Here I was, reading sexual text messages between my husband and his male "cousin." But how? How could my husband, who ravaged my body several times throughout the day desire a man? He didn't desire just any man, but a man who lived as a woman and considered themself a lesbian woman. *Yes—* he was a man with a penis, fake breasts bigger than mine, and a butt to put the latest IG models to shame. *Yes—* it was the man who he passed off as his

9

cousin for an entire year. He was the same one who nursed my wounds after surgery, attended our family gatherings, and even invited us to his birthday celebrations!

"Lorenzo, why did you chase me for three years to bring me here? How could you? Lord, Why me?" I screamed out to God as I fell to the floor in the greatest pain I'd ever experienced.

We coined it "A Baltimore Love Story." Lorenzo and I met at the grand opening of my school. I was the youngest principal to open a school in the heart of East Baltimore, and the entire community came out. I called it fate since I had my own DJ, but to get additional support from our partners, I had to agree to take on a group of Black male DJs. Who would turn that down? They came suited and booted — sharp brothers. The owner came over to introduce himself and shared that one of his partners was from the neighborhood. He couldn't wait to meet me. "You don't know Lorenzo Alston?"

"No, I don't." As I chuckled, a man parted the crowd and walked toward me with the biggest grin on his face. "Well, d@mn, who is this? I said to myself."

He extended his hand. "Hello, Ms. Debi, it's nice to finally meet you. I'm Lorenzo Alston."

Chile, I was starstruck for a quick second. The waves were spinning, and he was dressed to the nines. I thanked him for coming and walked away. After all, my boyfriend was about ten yards away from me.

James said, "Oh, I see you met Mr. Alston. Watch that n*gga. He thinks he's the smoothest n*gga in East Baltimore."

Oh, I was definitely watching him. "Why don't men of his stature ever pursue women like me?" was all I could think.

Months passed, and Lorenzo became a constant fixture in my school community. He hosted events, joined as the chair of my Parent Teacher Organization, and made sure I had tickets to all the premiere Baltimore events. I would always take my best friend with me so we weren't alone. After my boyfriend and I split, I considered dating him, but my best friend heard that he was a philanderer and that I shouldn't date him. Yet still, he would bring me lunch and come sit in my office for hours after school. We would talk about any and all topics, dreaming up grandiose ideas to transform the hood and his aspirations in politics. I supported his campaigns and even donned his gear in support. We were growing closer, but in my mind, men like him didn't date women like me.

I grew up in pretty challenging conditions, the child of an addict and another incarcerated parent. I spent most of my life battling uphill problems. But he was different. He had grown up in a two-parent household, retired from the military, and had just as many degrees as me. We would work rooms together, raise money for kids, and serve my school community until the wee hours of the night. Out of my desire for safety, I started seeing my high school boyfriend again. But Lorenzo was never too far away. He'd make sure he visited events every chance he got. He even started expressing how much love he had for me. But I was with D now. D was every bit of a G, a street guy who always protected me. After all, that's all I wanted— to feel protected, covered, and chosen for once.

One night we were watching the news, and Lorenzo came on the screen. D said, "There goes your man."

I started smiling and talking about Lorenzo a little more than I should have. D just looked at me. I wondered if I was in the right place at the time. I was sitting in my basement watching him smoke yet another blunt. What had my life become?

That week was my thirty-eighth birthday, and D planned to take me and my kids to dinner. What was supposed to be a night of fun and kindness turned into him being a Percocet-induced, bloody-nosed, raged man ruining my birthday. When we got back home from Virginia, I told him I had enough. I couldn't do this anymore. He was pissed, but he obliged. I had bought him a car with cash, and he allowed me to put a new car with a payment in his name.

In the weeks following our breakup, he would call me just to remind me that I had his car and that I needed to make sure I paid for it. "D, please, you're just trying to start some mess. I pay my bills. Leave me alone," was my constant reply.

After three weeks of back-and-forth, I was exhausted. Lorenzo came by my office with a bottle of wine to give in celebration of my birthday. I shared what had happened between me and D.

"D@mn, babe, that's messed up. I think I'm gonna have to make up for that," he said.

I was smiling on the inside. All I could think of was how he had so many women to choose from, and he was choosing me. Lorenzo asked to take me on a date to make up for my birthday, and I obliged. He even offered to pick me up.

I got super cute, and he called to say he was outside. I got outside, and he was in an old beat-up Pontiac Grand Prix. "Well," I told myself, "I guess he put all of his funds into the community." I hopped in, and we headed to DC for the Wizards game. He kept telling me we had box seats, but when we got there, we were in seats in front of the media box. I laughed to myself and didn't notice that this small white lie would become bigger lies.

The next day, Lorenzo called me and asked me if I had plans for the next weekend. I was with my best friend, and before I replied, I said, "I'm waiting on a check. Can you send me some money?"

He asked for my cash app and sent me $200. I was like "Girl, he sent me money," as if that was a major thing. He then said, "Since I passed your little test, can you go to the Pro Bowl with me next weekend?"

I jumped at the opportunity and traveled to Florida with this man. When we got to the hotel, he said, "I got double beds. I don't want you to think I'm not a gentleman."

I was in awe and was thinking to myself, "He is truly a gentleman."

We spent an amazing weekend together and came home making plans for more time. Over the next month, we hung out two to three times a week, and each outing included us partying nightly. I didn't notice it then, but Lorenzo always wanted to party whenever we weren't working.

Over the course of a month, Lorenzo shared with me that he needed to move out of his place. All his clothes were in his car, but he never told me he was homeless. I'd cook and he'd come and stay the night. My kids knew him over the years due to him being at the school and taking them on field trips, so they didn't trip about Mr. Lorenzo being over.

Lorenzo came over one day and said he found a place big enough for me and the kids. He wanted us to all be together, and since we had been friends for so long, I didn't think it was a bad idea. Aside from that, my ex (who I refer to as D), was constantly popping by my house and starting stuff.

Lorenzo and I moved in together at the end of February, and two weeks later, COVID-19 hit.

We were stuck in the house together.

For months, our days consisted of taking technology to kids' homes, giving out food to families, and delivering work packets. Our nights consisted of hanging out on the block with friends and family, partying, and talking trash. One night in particular, I was sitting on the steps of his cousin's house when a six-foot stallion came walking down the street— a body straight out of an IG sex post. As she got closer, I realized "she" wasn't a "she" at all. She was a man or, as politically correct terms would have it, a transwoman. "Hey, Lorenzo," she said.

Lorenzo said, "Oh hey, Chiquita, this is my girl, Mo."

I spoke and kept sipping my drink. As Chiquita walked away, Lorenzo started to give me more information than I asked for. "Oh, that's my cousin. She used to be a man. Everybody used to call her Faggy Mark, but now her name is Chiquita. Man, they are talking about her. She got a ten-inch d!ck and is getting girls pregnant. Word on the street is she doesn't take d!ck, but gives it."

I stared at Lorenzo, and all I could utter was "Oh, okay." I felt so uneasy, but it was his cousin.

Over the next few months, Chiquita was a constant fixture in our lives. She held a birthday party at her house, and Lorenzo hired a DJ and emceed the whole party. Chiquita and I danced together and even did a little dance around Lorenzo. Thinking back now, he had the best of both worlds right up under my nose. I had corrective breast surgery, and Chiquita told Lorenzo she'd take care of me while he worked. Chiquita was the very first person to visit me, fix me food, and change my drains. We were bonding, sharing surgery tips, and watching Netflix together.

That summer, we took a family vacation to South Carolina to visit Lorenzo's dad, Chuck.

Chuck was also a vet and a ladies' man. Lorenzo had shared with me that he was constantly trying to get him to give me a ring he had for someone else. Oddly enough, the fourth night we were there, Chuck called Lorenzo upstairs. Later that night, during a Pokeno game, Lorenzo proposed to me. I was so happy that I didn't even put two and two together, that I was being duped. Chuck yelled out, "Yeah, that Pro Bowl trip I gave you finally got you a wife!"

Months passed, wedding planning ensued, and our nightly partying episodes continued. I was drained, not functioning at one hundred percent, and trying to keep up with Lorenzo. He was always on the move, and a party was always on the horizon. My health took a toll on me, and I ended up really ill. I ran to the bathroom and vomited for about fifteen minutes. I started rumbling through the cabinets. My best friend had given me pregnancy tests and lots of medical supplies when we first moved in. Test after test came back positive. Oh my gosh— I was pregnant!

Lorenzo called me on the phone and inquired about why I sounded so horrible. He started a Facetime call. "Mo, talk to me, baby, what's wrong?"

"I'm pregnant, Lorenzo," I said.

I started crying, and he said, "Baby, I'm on my way."

We spent the next two weeks trying to decide what to do when he finally said to me, "I finally have the girl of my dreams, and now I have to share her with a baby." The decision was made. We were going to abort our baby.

The night before the scheduled abortion, Lorenzo went to fix me something to eat. As he was downstairs, I cried. For once, I had a man who had just as much chance at success as me. I loved him, and we were getting married. Why couldn't we have a baby? "I bet he's seeing someone else," I told myself. He would be gone for hours on end at times, and his shared location would say he was at the same East

Baltimore grocery store. I grabbed the phone. All I could think was that something wasn't right. As I went through his phone, something led me to his search history. I wasn't prepared for what I found. The titles read: "Swim Coach Gets Serviced by Hairy Big Black C*ck," "Teen Gets Banged in His A$$," "Tr@nny Edging," and "Man on Man C^m Fest."

As I scrolled, I could hear Lorenzo coming up the steps. "Baby, come on, let's get some food up in you," he said.

After we ate, our ritual of nightly sex started. He asked me to get on top of him. I looked down. "Lorenzo, are you gay?"

Lorenzo looked up at me. "What? What the h%ll are you talking about, Monique?"

"I found your porn history. It's all men f^cking men. Why are you watching these things?" Lorenzo took me off his body and said, "That wasn't me."

"Well, who the h%ll is it then because it's on your phone?"

He turned his back to me and turned the light off. The next morning, the ride to the abortion clinic was silent. He couldn't go in with me because of COVID-19 protocols. As I sat in the waiting room, all I could think about was the search history. "Is he gay? Is it just a fetish? Girl, you know d@mn well straight men don't watch gay porn. Are you being homophobic?" I texted him, "Baby, is this what you like? Please talk to me."

He said, "Babe, I watch it at times, but it ain't nothing. I only want you. I promise I won't look at that stuff again. Let's get through this baby thing together."

I swallowed the abortion pills and went out to the car.

The next two weeks were the most miserable weeks of our relationship. Lorenzo would be gone all day, claiming he was serving the community. He'd bring me food, drop it off, and kiss me on the forehead. After day four of passing our baby through an at-home abortion, Lorenzo wanted to have sex, and said he ain't scared of a little blood. I ended up with a bacterial infection so bad that my vagina was swollen shut. Even with the pain, Lorenzo would still want to have sex three to four times a day.

I went to the doctor, and my gynecologist said I had three strands of bacteria in my culture. She asked if I was wiping properly, as if my thirty-eight-year-old self didn't know to wipe from front to back. I assured her that I wasn't wiping improperly. Mourning the loss of my baby and feeling disconnected from Lorenzo pushed me further into work and hanging out on the block. We never talked about our dead baby again, and life went on.

We had the wedding of the century— two hundred seventy-five guests, twenty-six attendants, and a reception at the Ravens stadium. Now that I think about it, Chiquita wasn't at any of the festivities. Over the course of two months, I found out my fiancé had a baby the week I was aborting ours. He moved his fourth cousin and goddaughter into our house, and money ended up scarce. I incurred his debts. Here we were, two months into the marriage, and I was reading messages between him and his lifelong male lover.

Lorenzo snatched the phone from me, as I lay on the floor screaming. He said, "Get up!

Let's go outside." It was 3:00 a.m. We walked around the corner, and he sat on the church steps. "Lorenzo, don't think 'cuz we sitting on these church steps that I think you gone tell the truth," I said to him.

He replied, "Monique, you are the only woman I've ever loved, and I'm going to tell you the truth, baby."

I asked him matter-of-factly, "Lorenzo, are you gay?"

"No, I'm not," he responded.

"Lorenzo, do you f^ck men?" I asked him.

"No," he said.

So, I asked him one last question. "Do you f^ck tr@nnies?"

"Yes," he responded.

"Lorenzo, they're men! Chiquita has a d!ck!" I burst out.

At that moment, Lorenzo noticed a homeless person on the park bench across the street. He stood up and summoned me. "Come on, let's go home." We walked about ten feet, and he turned and said to me, "Make sure you wear comfortable shoes tomorrow. We have five events to show our faces at."

I went home and began my prayer journey. I took my children to my mother's house the next day, began looking for a place to live, and moved into my son's bedroom. I spent the next two months in our home alone. He would come in and out, but I didn't speak to Lorenzo, except to tell him I had drawn up a divorce agreement and the notary would come to the house.

During the notary visit, I asked Lorenzo if he knew why I was divorcing him. He said, "Yes, because I'm dishonest."

"No, Lorenzo, I'm divorcing you because you have sex with men. You put my health at risk. You didn't give me a choice."

This was the last conversation we had.

I spent the next year in a lot of emotional pain– drinking, partying, and running the streets. I was obsessed with my gynecologist's office. I took so many HIV tests that my doctor sat me down and begged me to stop. When I look back over the years of my adult love life, I can honestly say that my idea of a family and giving my kids what I didn't have blinded me. I thought having a partner was the completion of my covenant with God, so much so that I ignored the signs. I sought security, safety, and covering in man and not God. I didn't do my homework, and I avoided the red flags. I was adamant about making something work that shouldn't have even existed. My misalignment with God allowed me to make decisions that weren't blessed by Him. Thus, I suffered the consequences of being Monique-led and not God-led.

My weekly psychotherapy sessions uncovered the deep emotional scars that originated during my childhood. I am a people-pleaser, an "emotional stuffer," and believe that as long as I work hard to be a good girl, people will love me. I was able to finally understand why I didn't take the time to know this man deeply, didn't do enough research on him, nor ask the right questions. All I wanted was a family, and I accepted his outer shell as good enough to be in my world. I later discovered that I already had a family with my children, and that we had been fine all along. By taking these sessions, I started to learn what triggered me and started to pay attention to my physiological responses to stress. Processing emotion was not something I was ever allowed to do; I'd say that hurt and walk away from it. I'd been running my whole life– from myself! I also learned that I needed to take time to get to know a potential partner. Taking that time to work on me gave me peace that surpassed all understanding.

As a part of my healing journey, God led me back to Him. I started to consume Scripture daily, attend Bible Study, and connect with women who were on the right path. It took me a lot of time, and I'm still in the process of shedding old habits, learning what makes me happy, and overcoming the pain. My discernment is heightened; I view the world with new eyes. A part of me has always wanted to be accepted and revered by the world so much so that I became worldly. It took this deep pain and loss to help me discover that I am supposed to be who God designed, not what the world wants me to be. I set out to wear new wineskins that were handcrafted by God himself, not the shackles of the world. This fresh anointing has enabled me to truly understand Ephesians 3:20: "Now unto Him who is able to do exceeding abundantly above all that we ask or think, according to the power that works within us… to Him be glory in the church by Christ Jesus to all generations forever and ever." I had it in me all along. What I sought needed to be cultivated.

My life has done a complete 180-degree turn! I'm not hanging out in the streets all the time. I have deep relationships with my children, and I'm living a life of service. I started a support group for women who experienced a man living on the down low, and it has grown to support all women who just need sisterhood. It didn't happen overnight; I am still processing all of the emotions, and sometimes it's triggering. However, I didn't embark on this journey alone. My sisters in Christ, family, and friends have been here for me. God even sent me "my person" who has loved me, and forgiven me a lot through this healing journey. Sometimes, I'm not the nicest person, and sometimes I lash out at him. His level of patience and understanding are commendable.

My relationship with Jared guided me to put my focus on the only place it matters— on the Lord. Having a man in my life whose steps are ordered by the Lord was the icing on my healing cake. Jared has prayed with, for, and over me; he has helped me process my darkest emotions and has even incurred emotional abuse as a result of my trauma responses. But he hasn't left my side! He is honest with me and teaches me a new way. We study together and process our emotions in ways I didn't know were possible. I never knew this kind of love was possible, but I had to meet up with Monique to know it was real.

I often ask, "Lord, why me?" I recognize that it is because I am already saved. I am already saved by His Blood. It took such a traumatic event to wake me up to the understanding that God has laid the perfect foundation for me to create a legacy that I will pass down to generations to come. Without this darkness, I wouldn't know light. I am so grateful God kept me, held me, and uplifted me. If I can overcome it, you can, too!

* * *

My Word of Wisdom to You:

Sis, when you ask yourself, "God, why me?" know that you are God's beloved daughter. He loves you beyond measure. Sometimes, the painful lessons will become the very tapestry of your armor. You will use this armor to battle the worldly pleasures of your flesh in honor of the beautiful treasures God has embedded in you. Open your arms wide to the adversity and know that it is chiseling you into a beautiful masterpiece. The Bible says: "Do not be afraid , little flock, for your Father has been pleased to give you the kingdom" (Luke 12:32).

You are a woman in pursuit.

I AM AN OVERCOMER
DONIQUE LOMAX

Can you see it? Can you feel it? Just close your eyes and remember what it was like to be a kid with no worries, full of laughter and joy. Unfortunately, I won't close my eyes because the pain overflows the joy. I'm overwhelmed by flashbacks of rage, anger, and anxiety. I don't want to remember. But I can't forget.

I was eight years old when it first happened. I had just come home from the hospital. Yeah, I was that stubborn daughter who never wore shoes. On that day, my cousin was chasing me. Without thinking, I dashed out the front door and stepped on a screw. The pain I felt can only be described as something only God could understand. Naturally, my mom rushed over like the hero she has always been and pulled it out. But even she was concerned because of the amount of flesh that was stuck to the screw.

That same night, I was discharged from the hospital and heavily medicated. My mom allowed me to sleep on the sofa, since I couldn't walk up the stairs. When I woke up, I felt a heaviness pressing against my back, pushing me down. I could feel him inside. I began to cry because I couldn't comprehend why he would harm me. Upon hearing my tears, he leaped off and I sprinted upstairs, crying to my mom, but she couldn't hear me. She was exhausted. Waking her just seemed impossible. So, I curled up under her and cried myself to sleep.

The next day, she said, "I think I had a dream you were crying. Are you okay?" At that moment, I chose to lie and said, "Yes, I'm okay."

Now, my mom knew something was off because we shared everything. However, fear had taken hold of me; he compelled me to promise not to speak a word. I had never experienced fear like that before that day.

Then, when I was ten, it happened again. This time, my baby sister was fast asleep right beside me. We had drifted off while watching a movie. We went from laughing one moment to snoring the next. I awoke to that familiar weight pressing against me. But this time, I didn't shed any tears. That emotion had long disappeared before I even comprehended it, buried deep within and discarded. Instead, I rose from the couch because I couldn't allow him to shatter my sister the way he had shattered me. I lifted her and carried her upstairs. I held onto her tightly while he called out my name. I just knew that if I could get her to our room, she would be safe.

Once we got to the top of the steps, he came after us. I immediately ran into the bathroom, locking the door. Lea, my little sister, was so confused. She had no clue what had just happened, but I made sure to ask her all the right questions. I just needed to be sure he didn't touch her.

As we hung out in the bathroom, he stood by the door, apologizing, saying, "I'm sorry. I was just playing. You can't tell anyone about our game."

I was almost convinced that I signed up for this. I started to blame myself. Maybe the world was right about me. I was too friendly. Maybe I was promiscuous! I couldn't even spell that word back then. The remarks people made about me when I was a child, despite my innocence and free-spirited nature were getting harder not to believe. Gradually, I began to internalize them and believe them myself. Back then, it had me convinced that I deserved it.

About thirty minutes later, Lea and I climbed through the vent to our room and locked the door. My mom came home shortly after, and she asked me again, "Are you okay?" And I lied again. I said "yes." During this time, I was having nightmares and peeing in the bed. I was fighting every day. I couldn't focus on school. Things had gotten really dark for me at such a young age.

On July 4, 2001, I was watching the fireworks from my bedroom window. I was eleven years old at that time. Suddenly, I burst into tears and ran into my mother's room, crying. My crying was so intense that it made her cry, too. This time, she asked me, "What's wrong?" but I couldn't stop crying. She said, "Just tell me. I know you did nothing wrong." She lifted my head, looked at me, and said, "I need you to tell me." She began to pray, asking God to remove the fear and to allow her to hear me. There was a calmness that rested on me.

At that moment, I told her everything. I ripped the bandage off my infected wounds so my mom could be my NICU nurse. I was afraid she wouldn't believe me and that she would blame me. Fear had me convinced that my mom would be against me. However, I was wrong and foolish to ever think that way.

My mom took it really hard because she was overprotective. We could only travel in pairs, and staying over at someone's home was an absolute *no*. Only family was allowed around. My mom did everything right, but this still happened to me! She asked me if we could tell my sisters, and I told her "yes" because I didn't want them to feel ashamed or blame themselves for something they had no control over. I thank God that they weren't affected, but knowing that made me question God, "*Why me!?*"

At this point, my mom told her two big sisters and my sisters. I was cool with it because they all gave me a little strength. They all had their ways of encouraging me, actively showing me love, and praying with me. Somedays, my aunt and mom would grab holy oil and just start going in! Half of the time, I didn't even know what they were saying. But I knew they were talking to God on my behalf! I was angry with God. So, most times, I would just cry.

One summer day, I was at Aunt Gina's house playing. Both of my aunts and mom were there. I was outside playing with my sisters when I saw him walking down the street. Man, I flew into the house so fast. My heart was racing. This was the first time I'd seen him since I told my mom. The fear that came over me was unbearable. My sisters rushed in behind me yelling he's outside. After one look at my face, my mom knew what needed to be done. It was almost like she was prepared to go to war. Meanwhile, I was terrified!

My mom took me into Aunt Gina's bedroom while Aunt Gina went to get him. They brought him into the room with me. I squeezed my mother so tight, too afraid to look at him. It was like he was the devil himself. My Aunt Gina said, "We're right here with you."

My mother said, "This is when you take back what was taken from you." She lifted my head with so much strength and made me face him. She asked me if I had anything to say to him. As I held back my tears, I asked him, "*Why me?*"

He shook his head.

My mom looked me in my eyes and said, "He is just a pathetic man — a coward, a weak person. And there is no man on this earth you should fear. Not even the ones who hurt you! Look at him, he's more afraid of you!"

He was terrified. As he uttered the words, "I'm sorry," he already knew what my mom was capable of. Even though she wanted to cause him so much pain, God already assured her it was already done. My mom looked at me and gave me two options. At a young age, I had to decide whether to lie in my misery or fix my crown. My mom would say, "Fix your crown" often, so I knew what she meant. And I wanted to, badly, but I didn't have the strength, nor did I feel like I deserved to. So, my mom and my aunt stood me up. They anointed my head, my palms, and the soles of my feet with holy oil, as they spoke affirmations. They placed a crown so worthy of a queen on my head. I felt a sense of relief, but I also still felt broken.

It was at that moment that I realized God started to prepare me for my healing journey. Every day afterwards, I quoted Proverbs 31:25, while crying myself to sleep many nights.

"She is clothed with strength and dignity and she laughs without fear of the future."

— PROVERBS 31:25

Most nights, shame and guilt consumed me. It took me a few months to realize that wasn't enough, and that I had given this situation way too much power. At that time, I didn't believe that *"she"* in Proverbs 31:25 was me! But I started to put my name in it.

> *"Donique is clothed with strength and
> dignity and laughs without fear of the future."*

I had to remember to be kind and gentle to myself! I started writing little 'I love you' notes to myself. I had to stop dwelling on the trauma when God had already put me on the path of healing. He had already jump-started my process. But the flesh in me felt like I was supposed to be stuck. I was convinced this was who I was supposed to be— the victim— when God had already made me *victorious*! Once I understood that, I started asking God for everything I needed to rebuild myself.

I would randomly say to myself:

> "God, recreate in me a clean, pure heart. Build me up to be
> unapologetically bold in your name. Make my enemies
> my footstool. Allow my past to be my testimony."

God recognized the determination in my heart, and with His grace, I pressed forward every day. I no longer felt ashamed, guilty, or worthless. I wrote down every word I've been called— every name I believed to be true. I wrote them on a glass plate. Then, I threw the plate so far and hard that it shattered. That symbolized me breaking ties with those negative thoughts and feelings. I seriously had to forgive myself for being angry and blaming myself. I had to forgive myself for carrying all of those burdens for so long, just to later realize that they were never my burden to carry in the first place!

I thank God for the moment of awakening when I finally stopped carrying those burdens. That was when I started to feel free. My vision became so clear to me. I was at peace and felt love. There was no more crying at night! I was no longer burdened by a sense of disappointment. God completely set me free of the trauma that wanted to consume me. God gave me everything I asked for, plus some!

* * *

My Word of Wisdom to You:

To everyone reading my story, know that you can ask God for what you need in this season! Be intentional. Choose God completely and wholeheartedly. To this day, I still quote Proverbs 31:25 with my name in it! You can also do the same.

I'm sharing my story with you, not for pity, but to be a guiding light. I was fortunate enough to have God-fearing women around me who covered me; I had sisters who gave me strength when I had none. I urge you to get connected and lock in with some sisters on fire for God. Once you make a clear, conscious decision to walk the path that's waiting for you, your sisters are going to keep you covered. Love, itself, is going to break strongholds. Stand tall; you are not alone. Take your next step into your healing season! You've got this! All the glory goes to God!

You are a woman in pursuit.

Out of the huts of history's shame
I rise

Up from a past that's rooted in pain
I rise

I'm a black ocean, leaping and wide,
Welling and swelling I bear in the tide.
Leaving behind nights of terror and fear
I rise

Into a wondrously clear daybreak
I rise

Bringing the gifts that my ancestors gave,
I am the dream and the hope of the slave.
I rise
I rise
I rise

-Maya Angelou

I AM RESILIENT

EBONY MCCLENNY

G rowing up as a child, I was the youngest of three. I remember being my mom's "problem child." I wasn't necessarily a bad child, but I was always doing something I had no business doing. As a teenager, I began having sex at an early age, smoking weed with my friends, following the wrong crowd, and making bad decisions, at times. I got into fights at school and got suspended a few times, but I always maintained good grades. I was an honor student. I enjoyed learning, but I became rebellious at some point in my life. I didn't have a father growing up, and I began to search for love in all the wrong places. My mom was a heroin addict, and for a period of my adolescent years, I lived with my grandmother as my mom went to a rehab facility to free herself from her addiction.

My mom was a God-fearing woman. Even though she battled addiction, she raised us in church. She taught us how to pray, and we were forced to read scriptures and repeat them at night before bed. Those vivid memories of my childhood contribute to my faith in God today. Even though we were financially poor, we were rich in faith. I always wanted to have things my way, all the time.

One day my mom told me, "When you have children, you're gonna get it all back. One of your children is going to give you h%ll." I never really understood what she meant by that, but I later learned that from the Ten Commandments. One commandment that was very important to her was "Honor thy mother and thy father." She would often say, "If you do right, right will follow; but if you do wrong, wrong will follow."

I gave my mom h%ll during my teenage years. I later realized that I was angry with life. I didn't love myself the way I should have. I lived with guilt and shame from childhood experiences. I had to learn to forgive and let go of the past, especially if I wanted God to continue to bless me. I wanted to be a better woman, a woman of God, and one day a mom to my own children. Most of all, I wanted to be successful. I had a dream of owning a big house, driving a nice car, and experiencing the world differently. I didn't know what financial freedom looked like, but I wanted to feel a difference in what living in poverty felt like.

Most women envision life as a journey of big dreams. We visualize our success as being created from hard work and dedication, which ultimately drives us to become an unstoppable force. That success we wish to one day hand down to the next generation. To really enjoy the fruits of our labor and to watch our children inherit the joy of knowing my Mom paved the way is an indescribable feeling. That's what life is all about— reaching your success, fulfilling your God-given potential, and then passing the torch to the next generation so they may continue the cycle. Establishing that potential is sometimes hard to do.

As we go through life and face many obstacles along the way, many of us become overwhelmed, burdened, hopeless, relentless, discouraged, and often lose our faith in God. What you once thought your purpose was can sometimes become the reason to lose sight of the bigger picture. Then you begin to question, "Why me?"

My story began May 28, 2004, at about 12:02 p.m. That's the day I gave birth to my firstborn son. Weighing in at 5 lb. 10.2 oz., he was a little bundle of joy. Dakarai Malik Baldwin is what we named him. He was screaming, healthy, and had a head full of cold jet-black hair. Dakarai (which means "happiness" in Swahili) was named after his father's best friend who had been killed just months before I gave birth to him.

At just eighteen years old, I didn't know what to expect from parenthood. I had very few clues as to what to do. All I remembered was knowing I wanted to give my son a good life— a better life than what I experienced growing up as a child in a low-income housing development in Baltimore City.

I was a freshman in college, attending Coppin State University majoring in computer science at the time. I knew I had to make a choice, a sacrifice, which was to either stay in school or get a job to support my child. I decided to quit school and work full-time. Knowing that I had so many big dreams for my son, all I could think about was what I needed to do to fulfill them.

I had him christened at just three months old. I knew firsthand that he was covered by the Blood of Jesus when he entered this world. Shortly after that, I immediately began looking for my own place, although my mom didn't agree with me moving out of the house with an infant. Through the help of a program I was enrolled in for teenage moms, when Dakarai was about four months old, I moved into my very own place. It wasn't the best home, but it was mine, and I loved it. I decorated his room with Winnie the Pooh because he had received the entire set (stroller, car seat, high chair, playpen, etc.) at the baby shower. I probably had enough diapers to last an entire year, and his closet was filled from the ground up with clothing and shoes. Although my home was located in a West Baltimore public housing community, we lived exceptionally well. I promised myself I would relocate before my son was school-aged.

I would sometimes ask God, "Why me?" Why had I been chosen to be the mom of such a perfect baby? He was so handsome, so lovable, and so happy. I couldn't believe at times that he was my son. He was spoiled rotten, too. He was the first grandchild born on both my mom and dad's side of the family. He never needed anything.

His dad and I had a relationship for the first few months, but by six months old, his dad had been arrested and sent to prison for about eighteen months. After his release from jail and being home not even an entire year, he got into more trouble, causing him to be sentenced to twenty years in federal prison. Shocked, in disbelief, and full of emotions, I was not only scared, but also confused regarding how I was supposed to raise my firstborn on my own. My mom was a single parent, and that was always something I never wanted for my family. But here we have it, as the journey began of me raising my son on my own the best way I could.

By the time he was age three, I relocated my son and me to Baltimore County. A better neighborhood and school system were my decision-making factors, as I was house hunting. I didn't want my son to be exposed to the inner-city lifestyle. I refused to let him experience what struggle felt like. I dressed him in the latest designer clothes, and I kept him involved in every sport, from baseball to basketball to karate. Every summer, he attended sports camps and extracurricular activities to stay busy.

Being a mom was something I enjoyed. He had become my little rollie; he tagged along with me everywhere. I worked several jobs to provide the best for him, and by December 2008, Dakarai had become a big brother to my second son. He was so overprotective of "the baby" as he would always call him. At almost five years apart, they were total opposites. The baby (Raymond, Jr.) was a crybaby. Dakarai would often say, "Ma, why is my brother always crying? He wants me to play with him?" And that's just what he would do, play with him and read to him often.

As the years flew by, the two grew up inseparable. They were often fighting and feuding because Dakarai would often tease Ray and beat up on him (the typical sibling rival). They had different interests growing up. Dakarai was more a sports lover; Ray grew a love for electronics and computers. Dakarai kept me busy; between practices and sporting events, my weekends were very seldom free. I loved being a mom. The ups and downs and the highs and lows all taught me what was important. I learned to sacrifice what was sometimes not important in order to make sure my kids were always the main priority. Even though I had my times of struggle, my kids never felt it.

Christmas was always big, and birthdays were even bigger. As I remember as a child, we didn't always get the best, but my mom always made sure we had something. I remember the feeling of being poor, of not being able to afford the things we wanted, so I vowed never to let my children experience that feeling.

I think all moms have one thing in common, which is wanting the best for their children. I was very hard on both of my sons. Punishments usually consisted of lots of writing, extra chores, restrictions from games, no cell phones, etc. I would often tell Dakarai, "I'm only hard on you because I want the best for you." He was usually the one in trouble for something. I began to notice his aggressive behavior, which he tended to express during sporting activities. He would become very angry if he got a call from the referee or was reprimanded by the coach. I vividly remember one coach saying, "Nobody is going to want to coach you with that attitude." Dakarai, who was always a straight-A honor student, had begun to show signs of mood swings. I had numerous talks with him about his uncontrollable attitude, at times. But it became a frequent thing.

Over the years, he began to get into more trouble in school— not academically, but behaviorally. Suspensions, after-school detentions, and parent conferences happened more frequently. He didn't even care about being in trouble at a certain point in time. He would just shrug his shoulders, as if nothing bothered him. I started to relive my childhood, remembering all the trouble I put my mom through and her statement: "One of your children is going to give you h%ll." And boy oh boy, was she telling the truth. Dakarai was me all over again— a naïve adolescent who thought he had it all figured out.

All his teachers absolutely loved him. They often spoke highly of his ability to write great essays, his unique sense of humor, and his contagious smile. He left a mark on everyone he came in touch with, from schoolteachers to sports coaches and even childhood friends. Dakarai was a lovable and memorable child.

After countless encounters with the school authority during his middle school years, he made a very bad decision at the end of his eighth-grade year. His friend decided to bring a toy gun to school because they were filming a music video in the bathroom during lunch. That toy gun was seen by school officials, and Dakarai was expelled just a week before his eighth-grade graduation. I was livid with him. He was unable to participate in the closing exercises with his graduating class and was almost expelled from the entire Baltimore County school system. The one thing that saved him was his good grades and teacher-based references of his overall great work ethic. I had to meet with the superintendent of the school system, and he was luckily allowed to continue to the ninth grade but was not allowed to walk across the stage. He was punished for the entire summer because of this incident. He had to write every word in the dictionary and use it in a sentence. It's like punishments became a thing for him, and his nonchalant attitude didn't make it any better.

I prayed so hard for both of my sons every day, especially Dakarai. He always got a little extra prayer because what I noticed in him was a different path in life. I saw his eagerness to want to be indulged in negative behavior. Even after being in a Christian dance ministry for a few years, playing active sports since age six, and keeping straight As in school, Dakarai was changing. He started to become another kid, a kid who wanted to rebel, a kid who was seeking all the wrong attention. I didn't know what to do at a certain point. I was afraid of this path because I often told him he would end up dead or locked up if he continued these traits he possessed.

High School Years

In the fall of 2018, Dakarai was a freshman in high school. I couldn't believe how fast time flew. As parents, we literally watch our children grow right out of our laps and not even realize that we blink twice, and then they are grown. I was so nervous about him attending a school in the city because of their outstanding football team. His coach from the junior league requested some of his players come to the school to play for him. I agreed to let Dakarai attend with only one accord: he kept his grades up and didn't get into any trouble.

He did well in his first quarter, maintained honor roll, and was playing on the JV football team. But then he started to show aggression again. He hated being called out for his wrongdoings. The coach, who knew him from previous years, reached out to me, saying, "I don't know what's up with Dakarai, but he's not himself." He had gotten into trouble for shooting dice in school hallways, so the coach suspended him for one game. Dakarai was so mad that he turned his equipment in the next day and quit the team.

I couldn't understand how he would let one incident drive him away from something he loved and was so passionate about. I had talks with him about his behavior, but nothing changed. Things began to get worse. By the end of ninth grade, he showed signs of smoking weed, having sex, and running around with a totally different crowd of friends. I expressed my concerns with his dad through the mail and phone calls about how I thought our son was becoming another kid. I prayed more often. I would take him to church and force him to walk to the pulpit for individual prayers from the pastor. I worried that his behavior was leading him down a path of destruction.

Raising boys on my own had begun to take a toll on me. I often questioned, "What am I doing wrong? Why am I faced with this challenge? God, please help me figure it out." My firstborn son had become someone else, and I was losing hope on how to redirect him back to doing the right things.

By the tenth grade, I withdrew Dakarai from Mervo High School and sent him to live across town with his grandparents. That was a solution for getting him into a new environment with new friends and a better atmosphere. But little did I know, my son had already locked in with his crew that was involved in way more than I even imagined. They were carrying guns, selling drugs, and hanging in the inner city during the times I thought he was working and going to school. Baltimore is known as one of the most violent cities in the nation. Leading in over three hundred homicides a year, I feared that my son would one day be a statistic. I looked into military schools and camps, but most only started enrollment at age sixteen, and he was only fifteen.

A few months before his sixteenth birthday the world shut down due to the COVID-19 pandemic. So, there was very little to no hope for a solution, because no program was open to accepting new clients. I was stuck— stuck trying to figure out how to protect my son, who had fallen into a world of destruction.

By sixteen years old, my son was arrested and charged as an adult with a handgun and drug charges. We faced court date after court date, and he was sent to a juvenile facility in Eastern Shore, Maryland. After spending about ninety days there, he was released on home detention to finish the remainder of his probationary period.

I couldn't believe this had become my reality. My son who was once my athlete and straight-A student had now become a statistic, a criminal. He was now a number in the juvenile justice department. I talked to mentors and tried to enroll him in services, but he declined. He was very mischievous. He had very little to no regard for author-ity. He once told me, "Ma, you raised me right. I choose to do wrong." I cried many nights worrying about my son, praying for change. I fell into a state of depression. I beat myself up thinking I was a bad mother. My youngest son didn't give me any trouble at all, but Dakarai had turned into another person. I told him one day, "I don't even know who you are anymore. You are not the child I raised."

I continued to pray for my son. But he continued down the path of destruction. Although he worked, he continued to run the streets. He continued to hang around in troubled neighborhoods. He continued hanging out with friends who were not the best influence on him. I wondered where life would take him. I often told him, "You are going to end up dead or in prison if you don't change your ways." The reality was he had very little to no intentions of changing.

On Mother's Day, May 8, 2022, I told Dakarai, "The only thing I want for Mother's Day is for you to go to church with me." He agreed, and all three of us (he, myself, and Ray) headed to church that Sunday morning.

Just two weeks after Mother's Day, I received one of the worst calls of my life. It is the call every mother fears, especially when you know the lifestyle her child has been living. It was May 21, 2022, around 11:30 p.m. when I got that call. Dakarai, now just seventeen years old, had been shot multiple times, once in the head. I was very calm for some reason. I remember closing my eyes, saying, "Lord, give me strength."

As I headed to the hospital, I could hear his voice in my head. I relived all the arguments and long talks about this one day happening to him. I prayed as I headed to Johns Hopkins Hospital.

After waiting, what felt like hours for the doctors to come outside of the emergency room, I was finally called inside and given the devastating news. Dakarai was fighting for his life. He had very little to no brain activity, and the only thing that could be done was to place him on life support for comfort. I was heartbroken because my pain had become a reality— the pain of knowing that street life would one day possibly take my son away from me. Hit with guilt, shame, and other emotions, all I could do was continue to pray.

I received an outpouring of love and support. Family and friends gathered at the bedside as we prayed, we cried, but ultimately, I mentally prepared to bury my firstborn son. Seventeen years of life flashed before my eyes. That handsome little bundle of joy that I carried in my womb for nine months was now lying on his deathbed. Speechless, hopeless, and unable to think straight, I went to church the following morning. As I stood at the same pulpit just two weeks prior, I broke down, got on my knees, and asked the congregation to pray for my son as he was fighting for his life. Members of the church were devastated. They all offered support, as I emotionally fell apart.

After five days on life support, Dakarai succumbed to his injuries. He gained his wings on May 27, 2022, just one day shy of his eighteenth birthday. My son didn't live to see eighteen. It was a total shock facing the reality that he was really gone forever.

Why me? I would never understand why God used me to be a vessel. It was so unreal, but I continued to push myself every day. I prayed and I cried. I cried and I prayed. I began to believe God had a path for my life, which was to save others who were like my son. As I tried to understand grief, depression took over. Some days were better than others, but ultimately, I managed. You learn to manage as you cope with loss.

Why me? God knew I was one of his strongest soldiers on the front line. He needed a survivor to tell her story. He needed a true warrior to fight 'til the end. That's me, I'm a survivor, a true warrior who has a battle to overcome.

As I still struggle today with the pain of losing a child, I often find that this pain has a purpose. My son's death was not in vain. He was a Child of God. He was covered by the Blood of Jesus, and because of that, his soul had a beautiful transition into heaven's gates. I've struggled many nights sleeping and wondering if I could have or should have done things differently. My faith in God is what keeps me going, and then I remember, God makes no mistakes. My son was chosen. His story will change many lives and touch many hearts. I promise to keep his name alive.

I started a nonprofit organization in remembrance of my son. I named it SON Organization. SON stands for Surviving Our Neighborhood. I look to be a voice for other mothers going through what I went through. My mission is to encourage the youth, inspire the youth, and build healthy relationships at home so parents can learn how to cope with emotional and mental trauma caused by grief. We face challenges every day, but with God's grace, we can overcome anything.

* * *

My Word of Wisdom to You:

If you've ever lost a child, turn your pain into purpose and trust God. Yes, it's a challenging process marked by unimaginable grief and heartache. However, amidst the darkness, turning your pain into purpose can become liberating for you and others. This transformative process involves finding meaning amid despair and allowing the memory of your beloved child to become a source of inspiration for positive change.

It is my hope that you can discover a renewed sense of purpose, and learn to trust God beyond your deepest sorrows. Don't give up, no matter how hard it seems. Continue to live.

You are a woman in pursuit.

I AM FREE

ALICIA SMITH

hy me? That's a good question. The more I think, the more I ponder. Why, *really*, me? I try to do right by everybody. I try to live right. Am I not good enough? Why does stuff always happen to me?

I often reflect on my childhood; how could I not? I became pregnant during my 12th grade year. I was carrying a beautiful baby girl named Ki'morah. The journey started with a gender reveal, filled with smiles and shopping for cute outfits, blushing with excitement. But then, it took an unexpected turn. I found myself devastated, screaming in pain, kicking, crying, and enduring crucial contractions.

At five months pregnant, I went into labor. A lot of mixed emotions surfaced all at once. All I knew was that I was scared, but when it was time to give the doctor two big pushes and Ki'morah was born, I watched as life was taken away from me and my baby girl. She took one breath, and God took her home. It hurt me to my core; my heart was shattered. I could recall feeling lost, clueless, emotionless, and vulnerable— wondering why this happened.

I was young and couldn't decipher all my feelings. I simply knew that I wanted to be alone or be wherever she was. I wanted not to feel. I didn't understand why I had to go through this. I had never experienced heartbreak before. I never wanted to feel like that again. I was depressed and didn't eat, sleep, or bathe. I was out of my mind. I was down for a while, and it was the support and strength from my family that truly kept me going. There's no greater pain than losing your child. I thought Ki'morah was sent to give me life, purpose, joy, and happiness. That loss brought everything but that: numbness, bitterness, anger, betrayal, and more.

Speaking of betrayal, while going through a loss, thirty days later, I found out that Ki'morah's dad had another woman pregnant. I mean, really, out of all times, right? That baby was a spitting image of him, and he couldn't deny her. Of course, he denied her for five years. But because I lacked self-respect, self-love, integrity, and self-worth, I stayed for seven long years with him.

So there I was, holding a man down who didn't deserve the good woman I was. I was raised right, so I knew how to take care of my man. I knew how to stay when times got tough. However, I didn't realize that every year I stayed with him allowed me to lose value in myself. I was in denial.

I was twenty-one years old with a man who wouldn't even accept his own child (by another woman), but claimed he still loved me. He couldn't be honest, came and left out whenever he wanted to, couldn't keep a job, and the list goes on. He brought nothing to the table and added nothing to my future. I was the breadwinner for the majority of the relationship and overly loyal for the entire seven years we were together. I knew it was time for me to find my exit strategy. I had a problem with letting go, but in that seventh year, I left him.

All along, I was working my way to a better life and a "better man," or so I thought. The pain I carried in my heart was like no other. I lost my baby, Ki'morah's dad betrayed me, and then he had a baby with someone else. I eventually started feeling stupid. How could I stay all that time accepting the faults, failures, lies, and the cheating? Why was I settling? I don't know, but from then on, all I knew was I'd never trust again. I just needed to fill a void; I wanted to feel free again. I had been through enough, I would say. But it was just the beginning!

After leaving that relationship at twenty-four, I became numb to pain, guarded from all emotions, and hard-edged. I didn't want commitment; I was scared to feel vulnerable. My friends would call me Leo instead of Lee; they felt I was a "n*gga at heart," in their words. I wasn't affectionate or romantic; I was not in touch with my feminine side. My vibes with my boyfriends looked more like a homeboy and a homegirl— a brother-sister type of vibe— but still caring, loving, loyal, supportive, and inspirational. That was just me being naturally myself, or so I thought. I gave love like no other; I just didn't feel I was capable of being loved, so I never fully locked in.

However, I did end up dating a "boy toy." I was his crush since he was fourteen. We both are now grown. I never liked him the way he liked me, but he was something familiar to me. He wined and dined me. He was a "yes" man and got me everything I wanted. I never knew what "no" sounded like when he was around me. He would call me his dream girl. However, I knew it was too good to be true. At the time, being with him was a void that needed to be filled, so I didn't care.

Despite how well I was treated in this new relationship, I found myself going back to deal with Ki'morah's dad. I felt like he needed me. I allowed him to get in my head and make me feel bad about how I just got up and left him. But once me and my "boy toy" moved in together, I kicked Ki'morah's dad to the curb. He was out of sight and out of mind. Although I was all into my new relationship with my "boy toy," I was still guarded. I didn't play around. I was prepared to walk away without going back. If anything felt like betrayal or dishonesty, I was ready to leave. You could call me a pack and play.

Boy, did I ever pack and play! Moving forward, you might think I'd catch a break after the initial blows in my early 20s. But here I am, living my best life in my mid-20s, around 23 or 24, with my own house, car, no kids, traveling, and bringing in about 5k a month - that was a big deal for me at the time. Plus, there was extra money for me to splurge; me and "boy toy" were doing well. I hardly even knew what downtime was like, especially since we were both Leos with a hustling mentality that kept us going. I didn't need another man for anything; I even felt comfortable enough to let my guard down for a little while. I was happy with "boy toy" who loved me more than I loved him; there was no way I could get hurt. Yeah, right, as I mentioned before, it seemed too good to be true.

The enemy turned up the heat, but everything changed when a girl approached me, claiming she was pregnant by "boy toy" who was supposed to be my prince charming, the "too good to be true" man I had been dealing with for two years. This time, I knew what to do—get myself out of that situation. I wasn't going to let another year slip away from me, so I started dating someone else immediately.

Three months into dating a new guy, my previous partner, who I playfully referred to as my "boy toy," still gave me money, and I would accept it. We were still in contact, but I needed some space. Unfortunately, my previous partner didn't handle that well. One day, he saw a photo of me with the new person I was dating on social media— a post shared by a close friend. Looking back, I realized it was a foolish move on my part.

I was aware of how possessive and obsessive some of my previous partners had been, so I knew the last thing they needed to see was me with someone new so soon. This revelation upset him greatly. Within seconds, it seemed like my previous partner (who I referred to as "boy toy") was at my front door. I had been asleep when he arrived, a bit intoxicated from a night out, so I was initially cautious. However, as the banging and yelling continued, it became clear that something was happening in my living room, and I was fully awake and alarmed.

I quickly got up and entered the living room. It was my previous partner ("boy toy"), sliding the window open and urging me to open the door. He was yelling and saying, "Pooh, open the door!" I shook my head, thinking this was too much, and that he wasn't usually like this. But then, I saw him cocking a gun, and I yelled in shock. I knew this was unnecessary; he wasn't usually like this.

I walked in circles, talking to myself, trying to gather my thoughts. I told myself, "Lee, you've got this. Just tell him you'll talk to him another time and get this new guy out of your house." It was the first time I had ever felt such anxiety. I instructed the new guy to stay right there, assuring him that everything would be okay and that he didn't need to feel threatened.

I stepped outside, and when I looked back, I saw my short, cocky guy (my new guy) right behind me, ready for action. I thought, "Okay, let's all just calm down. I'll talk to you at a better time," I said to my new guy.

But suddenly, my previous partner ("boy toy") started walking towards me, attempting to grab my arm. I couldn't believe he did that. Then, out of nowhere, he pulled out a gun. I couldn't help but wonder, "Why me, God? What is happening?" I asked him to put the gun away before he ended up in jail, reminding him that we were surrounded by cameras. It wasn't worth all this trouble. However, when I turned around, "boy toy" had disappeared without a trace.

At this point, I was still disoriented and still a bit drunk. My only goal was to get the new guy in my house out of there and drop him off. We had only been involved for nearly two months, and he went to the extremes! I didn't sense any harm; it seemed like he just wanted to prove a point to me because you could clearly see that he was sensitive. As I drove him home, two police cars pulled up behind me. Anxiety surged again because I knew what was in the car. Before the officers could even get out, my new guy threw a gun onto my lap and told me to hide it since there were no female cops around. I looked at him in disbelief, feeling that sudden betrayal when you've trusted someone enough to have them in your personal space. This wasn't child's play; I didn't know how to process it. I had no control, and I was scared; anxiety consumed me.

All I knew was that this new guy had the wrong idea entirely. I unleashed my frustration, not caring that the police were approaching the car. I tore into him, unable to believe what he had just done.

When the officers arrived at the car, they said they received a call about a gun being present. The gun was still visible, protruding from under the seat. I knew they could see it. I couldn't believe what was happening. He quickly explained to the police that it was my ex-boyfriend's gun. My heart sank. They decided to handcuff both of us.

As I got out of the car, I asked what was going on, but they weren't forthcoming with answers. As I was placed in the police car, I started having a panic attack. I struggled to breathe properly. From a distance, "boy toy" saw me getting arrested for something I knew I had nothing to do with.

This hurt was different from the cheating and betrayal I had experienced before. I felt like I was being dragged through the mud by both parties simultaneously. My back was against the wall, and I didn't know who to call. All I could think to say in the back of that police car, all the way to the precinct, was "Jesus, Jesus, Jesus, Jesus, Jesus, Jesus." I kept repeating it, asking God what He was trying to show me. I couldn't help but question, "God, I know you wouldn't do me like this. What did I do?" All I could do was talk to the Man upstairs. He kept me sane; I felt like I was on the brink of losing my mind. Some of the leadership at the jail urged me to take the gun charge, but it was overwhelming. I couldn't call my family, and during those three days I spent there, it was just me and God.

I didn't eat or talk; I was just trying to hear from God. It was during this time that I felt He told me He uses His chosen ones to go through the toughest battles for a greater purpose. I didn't fully understand it then, but I knew I had to extract a lesson from what was happening this time. It was unbelievable, and I always knew God looked out for me, but during this ordeal, my faith wavered a bit. Eventually, they released me on my own recognizance on Monday morning.

I may not have fully understood why I was experiencing the challenges I faced, but I always believed they were part of a larger plan. I ended up fighting the charges for a year. The new guy and I became co-defendants, and he repeatedly tried to persuade me to take the blame, but I refused every time. I believed in standing up for what was right because if you don't stand for something, you'll fall for anything.

While I was fighting the charge in 2019, I decided not to date and remove friends who weren't supportive. I isolated myself from almost everyone. My emotional state was good, and things seemed to be going in my favor in court until life threw me another curveball.

I showed up to court dressed in my Sunday's best, confident that my record and background were clear. It was evident that it was the new guy's gun, but because I didn't explicitly mention his name in court, the judge ruled against me. I was sentenced to ten weekends in jail and two years of probation, effective immediately. I was devastated. I had never been to jail. I couldn't believe this was happening to me. I kept thinking, "God, why me? I thought you had my back. What went wrong? I've distanced myself from everyone, changed my habits, and tried to do right by people. What's happening?"

I ended up completing eight weekends instead of the initially imposed ten due to good behavior. Eventually, I was able to take my case back to court and was fortunate to get a positive outcome. On April 16, 2023, my record was expunged. Yes, I had to endure some bumps, blows, heartbreaks. I faced challenges like not being able to find a job in my field for three years, the loss of a child, and some mental disturbances. But looking back, I wouldn't change a thing.

Everything I went through shaped me into the woman I am today. I can now walk with my head held high, fully aware of who I am. I've stopped seeking validation in my relationships. I know what I want in life. I've realized that I can't afford to invest in pointless relationships, and I can't control every aspect of my life; sometimes, I need to let things happen. I've learned to choose those who choose me and to put an expiration date on loyalty when it's not reciprocated.

I've come to understand that self-love is the foundation for how others will love and respect me. Equipped with these tools, everything else falls into place. My relationship with God is unlike any other; He is a daily presence in my life. I've discovered that when you prioritize God, He provides abundantly. You will want for nothing; God will grant you what people say you're not qualified for. With Him, failure isn't an option, and I can't imagine life without Him. He will never abandon you.

I've realized that it's more important to have a close relationship with God than to focus on finding a mate or friends. When you make Him your best friend, He'll send remarkable people into your life—people with pure hearts who will bless you just because. So, when I reflect on why I went through all of this, I understand that it had to happen. I know that many women couldn't walk in my shoes, and I couldn't walk in theirs. It's important to be willing to share your story;

it's your testimony, and you never know how many lives you might touch, even if it's just one.

Each one should reach one; God made us all different in His image, and we all have a purpose. The goal is to tap into that purpose and not allow life's hardships dictate your future. They are merely obstacles we have to overcome. Don't lose hope, faith, or courage.

> "He heals the brokenhearted and binds up their wounds. He deter-
> mines the number of the stars and calls them each by name. Great is
> our Lord and mighty in power; his understanding has no limit. The
> LORD sustains the humble but casts the wicked to the ground."

> — PSALM 147:3-6

After years of dealing with trauma and embarking on my healing journey, God opened up a new dimension in my life. The things I used to enjoy, the places I frequented, and the people I saw myself with no longer held any purpose. It became clear that God was trying to reveal my purpose to me, but I kept getting distracted and unintentionally blocking my own blessings. He didn't want certain people in my life because they didn't align with what He had planned for me. He wanted to offer me His peace of mind and show me that healthy relationships still exist. However, He needed me to trust Him more and commit fully to His guidance. He wanted me to eliminate all distractions, whether they were relationships, friendships, or habits.

After two years of therapy and reestablishing my spiritual relationship with God, I began to close doors that needed to remain shut. My life underwent a complete transformation. I now have a beautiful four-year-old daughter and work as a behavioral specialist. I started a mentoring group for girls and serve as a mentor and coach. This group focuses on essential life lessons such as self-love, integrity, values, self-awareness, knowing one's identity, being discerning with trust, and choosing friends wisely.

Everything I was taught and everything I've learned from my personal experiences, I now impart to the youth, my peers, my daughter, and my family. By healing and trusting God to mend my broken heart, I've broken generational curses. While I may not have answers to all my "whys," once I discovered my purpose in life and learned who I truly am, I thanked God for choosing me.

* * *

My Word of Wisdom to You:

It's essential to let go of what you can't handle and allow God to take control. He doesn't make mistakes, and you are not defined by your past. Life often presents us with challenges, burdens, and situations that are beyond our control and capacity to handle on our own. It's vital to recognize that as human beings, we have limitations. We can't always fix everything or carry every burden alone. We must surrender to God. This act of surrender is not an admission of weakness, but an acknowledgment of humility and a way of expressing faith in His divine plan.

Lastly, always remember that your past does not define you. Regardless of what you've been through or the mistakes you've made, you have the capacity for growth, transformation, and redemption. By releasing the weight of your past, you allow yourself to move forward unburdened by guilt, shame, or regret.

You are a woman in pursuit.

I AM CHOSEN

SHERRITA COATES

My mother got pregnant by a man who she didn't know was recently married. She told him she was pregnant, and he denied paternity. She was young with one child and now another on the way. She decided an abortion would be the best decision. My mom heard about the upcoming concert of Bishop Jackie McCullough, a well-known preacher who had spoken throughout the US, Asia, Africa, Japan, Jamaica, who was now coming to Baltimore. My mother had to be there! She went to the concert at the church where Bishop Jackie McCullough called her out of the crowd. The Bishop said, "This baby has a calling on her life! The devil is trying to attack her vision! The baby is blind, but God said for everyone in this building to pray for the baby's sight! He also gave me instructions to lay my hands on your belly, and He will restore her sight!"

He did, too! Word spread quickly in the family about the upcoming abortion. A family friend reached out to my mother with an offer she couldn't refuse. She and her husband wanted another baby girl. She requested, "Can you have the baby and give her to us? We will be her godparents so you can still receive money from the state to help you get on your feet. We will take good care of her for free. We will raise her as our own. Let's be clear that when you give her to us, you can't take her back. You can see her anytime you like and even get her on weekends, but she's ours." My mother agreed, until she had me and saw me in the flesh. I was beautiful with a head full of hair, big cheeks, and chinky eyes with vision problems. The doctor said, "Ma'am, there's a possibility that your baby may become blind." At this time, my biological mother wanted to change her mind about giving me up.

However, two weeks after my birth, she gave me up. Living with my godparents, I received the best of the best. I was a goddaddy's baby, too! My goddad watched me while my godmom worked. My godmother got me anything I wanted. I had very nice clothes, shoes, socks, and games. I also attended private school. However, all I wanted was my biological mom. I couldn't wait for Fridays to hang out with my biological mom. She was so much fun! My mother would always make me laugh. She was known as the fun aunt. She would always have my cousins over and do fun stuff with us. She didn't have much, but what she had made me feel so special— unconditional love! She would give me paper food stamps and take me to the market to get a bunch of goodies. Every evening at 5:00 pm, we would feed the birds one loaf of bread. On Sunday evenings, I would get sad waiting for my goddad to pick me up because I knew I had to go back home. I would beg my biological mom to keep me. She would say she couldn't afford my lifestyle and send me back. After the quiet ride home, as soon as I'd walked through the door, my godmother would take all the snacks out of my hands and say, "We share in this house." She didn't understand that taking the only things my biological mother could afford to give me hurt me each time! Both mothers (biological mom and godmother) couldn't get along for anything once I was born. They would go back and forth, not knowing they were really hurting me! They even had a fistfight in front of me! I learned quickly good and bad from both environments. I saw how it was to have a two-parent household. Then, I saw how hard it was to have a single-parent household.

My godparents didn't have the best marriage, but when they got on one accord, you better watch out! My godmom was strong, purpose driven, and stern. I saw how she set goals and accomplished them. She always had a plan B in place just in case plan A didn't work, so I learned quickly. I remember being six years old and seeing my mother struggling, so I felt that I had to help her. By this time, my biological mom had another child, so I would help feed, change, and burp him, just to make things easier for her. My godparents had each other, my grandparents had each other, but my biological mom had no one! For years I begged my biological mom to keep me, and of course, she would say she couldn't afford my lifestyle. I didn't care about the material things. All I wanted was to help my biological mom.

Little did I know, my biological mother contracted HIV from her boyfriend who, in my eyes, she didn't take time to know before sleeping with him. By the grace of God, my brother didn't contract it in the womb. For years, I had constant flashbacks of how she would introduce her boyfriend to her close circle. I remember the lust in her eyes and in theirs when they saw him for the first time. They would say, "Oh, he is gorgeous!"

After a while, he couldn't hide his drug addiction. She was able to get rid of him, but now, she was HIV positive!

Although both houses were extremely different, one thing was the same! Both mothers knew the Lord! We always went to church and we always prayed, which I enjoyed!

At age nine, I had a dream that changed my life. I was in heaven along with my cousins from my generation. They were playing on slides, swings, etc. I was the only one sitting on a cloud crying! Jesus approached me and asked, "Why are you crying?"

I replied, "Because I want to live with my biological mother!"

He said, "Well, you know you can't live there!"

I said, "Well, you are Jesus! You can do anything!"

He laughed and said, "For you, I will do it!"

I started falling through the sky, and I woke up. I packed my bags and asked my godmom, "Can you take me to my biological mother's house? I want to live with her!"

Of course, that made her upset! I got punished for two days. I was determined to leave, especially after that encounter with Jesus! My bags were packed, and I was waiting. At the end of day two, I overheard my godparents talking. My godfather said, "Let her go! She's used to the finer things in life. She will be back!"

My godmother stormed into my room and said, "I'll take you, but don't you take anything I bought you!"

I looked down, and the only thing she didn't buy me was a pair of tennis shoes my biological mother bought, not knowing my shoe size. I said, "The only thing you didn't buy are these, but they are too small."

She said, "Walk on the back of them."

That hurt me to my core, and to this day, it still stings! My godmother dropped me off, and I was happy to be with my biological mom. We praised the Lord for hours! We were *so* happy! I never forgot that moment because that was the Friday I moved in with my biological mother.

On Saturday, reality hit me. I had nothing! My godparents cut me off financially, I guess to teach me a lesson. My biological mother said, "I told you I couldn't afford you! If you ask for anything, I'm sending you back!" I was so hurt that my God mom's love came with conditions, but I understood.

I just asked, "Well, can I wear your clothes and shoes?"

She said yes! I went from wearing a size 4 shoe on Friday to wearing size 8 shoes on Sunday. She put me in school where I was teased for the holes in my clothes and big shoes. The electricity got cut off. By this time, my older brother was out of the house. My biological mom had no food, and she was sick. I started noticing visible changes in her appearance. She started losing weight. Multiple tumors developed behind her right ear, causing her to lose hearing. Her skin was discolored, and she was laying around more. When I would ask her to get a job, she would say, "I'm sick!" Then, I would reply," How long is it going to take for you to get better?" She would just stare at me. I didn't understand the magnitude of how sick she was because she hid her diagnosis from me. I just didn't understand why she wasn't trying to get a job and provide for us. I had a two-year-old brother, and I knew if I didn't figure out how we would eat, we wouldn't eat. Around this time she took me to my paternal grandmother's house to meet her. My grandmother looked at me and said, "She looks just like me! I know this is my grandchild. Let me call my son!" At the same time, she called my brother down the steps to meet his little sister. As we hugged, I could hear my grandmother fussing with her son; then she hung up. This must've made my biological mother upset. My grandmother said," My son is saying this isn't his child, but I know she is because she looks just like me. I don't care what he is saying. Can I still be in her life?" My biological mother replied, "Since he's saying she's not his, you can't see her anymore!" Then, my mother grabbed my hand and said "Come on Sherri, let's go!" My grandmother teared up, as we walked out the door. I was thinking to myself, "I'm ok with him not being in my life because I already have a father, but I really want to know my grandmother and siblings." I also figured that she may help us, but now it's all on me!

I started going to school, brainstorming ways to steal food; eventually, I started stealing food every day to feed my family and me! I wouldn't do classwork because all I could think about was how hungry we were. I joined an after-school program because they gave me two snacks. I would go home and split the food three ways to feed us. On the weekends, I would take my brother to a neighborhood classmate's house to eat because his mother would feed us. Eventually, he told the children in my school, so I stopped coming over to eat. I even sometimes picked up the phone to call my godmother, but then I would hang up! I knew if I told her, I would never see my biological mom again.

I ended up failing the fourth grade. I remember crying to my biological mom, and she said I needed to repeat the grade because I had a hard time learning. I was thinking that maybe if I didn't have this adult responsibility, I could just be a kid and do well in school. The work was so easy, but I was in survival mode!

By age ten, we were homeless. We were getting kicked out of shelters by the day, and I didn't understand why. Back then you couldn't have a disease and live in a shelter. We would walk for hours in the heat with big bags on our backs. My biological mom would cry to me, "Sherri, where are we gonna stay?"

I would reply, "Don't worry, Ma! God got us."

He did, too! We ended up at this shelter where the owner slipped up and said, "How long have you been HIV positive?"

I couldn't believe my ears! My biological mother looked at me and said she didn't know! They put me out of the room. I was in the hallway now, understanding why things were the way they were. The owner felt so bad that she was able to get my mother into a transitional housing program where we had to live in a school building for one year, and after a year, she would receive support from Section 8 Housing.

By this time, I was able to talk to my godparents. I was able to go to their house where I saw my belongings distributed amongst the other children. It was Christmas. As the children opened their gifts, I had nothing. That's when I knew I wasn't their responsibility anymore. My goddad felt bad, and from that moment, we stayed in contact. He would always pop up at my house to visit me, but he had no money to give me. Psalm 27:10 spoke to me so clearly and stuck with me. It says, "Though my father or mother forsake me, the Lord will receive me." I knew that I was God's child.

At age twelve, I was walking home with a group of children from my school that I didn't know too well. I ended up being shot in the eye with a paintball, but I wasn't the intended target. My biological mom and godparents came together for me during this situation. I was happy to see them getting along, despite the circumstances .My maternal grandmother made me get on the news where I was humiliated! People would see me and laugh. I lost total vision in that eye. My right eye was crossed from the injury, and my pupil was torn. I had to go to a specialist every day for a month. On the thirtieth day, I was scheduled to get a glass eye. I got used to people laughing at my eye.

On the twenty-ninth day, I saw a neighborhood girl who all the young girls respected. When she saw me, immediately, she cried! She said for me to go into the house because she didn't want to see me like this. I walked into the house. My mom was in the kitchen. I said to myself, *If God isn't in any other part of this house, I know He's in my mother's room!* I went straight upstairs to her room. I closed the door and cried out to God. I said, "Lord, I don't want a glass eye! I'm too young! I have my whole life ahead of me!" Then, I fell asleep.

The next day, as soon as I opened my eyes, I knew God healed me before I even looked in the mirror! I could see out of my right eye again!

My mom took me to the specialist. He couldn't believe that my eye was healed because he had just seen me yesterday, and I didn't have vision in that eye. He asked in disbelief, "What did you do?"

I said, "I prayed!"

He said, "Well, by the time you are thirty years old, you will lose vision in that eye."

I didn't receive what he said because I knew the God I served!

Now I was a teen and trying to comprehend the fact that my mother was dying from HIV. On my thirteenth birthday, I felt like I was twenty-one because of all the responsibilities I had. My family looked down on me. They really didn't know me and prejudged me. I was labeled trouble, just like Jabez. The family wouldn't want me to talk to their children because they thought I was a bad influence. They would call me names like fast because I had a boyfriend when I really wasn't fast at all. I figured since I don't have their support, I'll keep this boyfriend, so when my biological mom dies, he can be of some support. It really hurt me how they would act towards me.

By this time, my biological mother lived for God. She ate the Word night and day! If you saw her, she always had the Word of God in her hands. My mother was so easy to talk to, so I talked to her about everything. I would even cry to her about the way the family treated me during family functions. She would say, "Sherri, your friends are your family!" She was right, they became family!

Before I left the house, my mother would pray over me. She knew that once I walked out those doors, she was turning me over to God. Let me tell you, He was showing up. I never was a drinker, but I smoked weed occasionally. Things would happen to my friends as soon as I left! Time and time again, I knew it was my mother's prayers that protected me! It started scaring me because I couldn't hide from the Lord. One particular friend started noticing the protection when I came around, too! My mom was so close to God that any spirit I carried by the time I entered the door would leave. She was a prophetic seer, so God would allow her to see things before they happened.

Little did I realize, I was a seer too! God spoke to me very clearly and said, "You can't serve two masters." So, I asked Jesus to change me, and He did.

When I turned sixteen, my biological mom's hair started thinning out. She got so skinny. I came home and opened the door and saw her stretched out on the floor. I called one of my great-aunts who happened to be in the area. We took my biological mom to the emergency room, and she told them she was HIV positive. The doctor came back in and said so coldly, "Well, it has turned into full-blown AIDS now!"

My biological mother fell in my arms crying. I couldn't believe what I just heard! My aunt let that doctor have it because he clearly had no compassion. Although my biological mother was weak, she decided to go back to school and received her High School diploma. During this time, my mother started asking me to have a baby. She also asked my older brother. She said, "I just want a granddaughter before I die."

Guess what? I ended up pregnant at the age of seventeen. I was so young and didn't want a child, and neither did my off again-on again boyfriend.. I had an abortion scheduled for Saturday. When I came into my biological mother's room on Wednesday, the radio was on talking about abortions. I felt convicted! I told my mom, and she said to have the baby and give the baby to her. Halfway through my pregnancy, my older brother was expecting a baby, as well! My mother was so excited that her grandchildren were on the way. She said, "Whoever has a girl, I will be so happy!"

My brother thought he and his girlfriend were having a girl, and I thought I was having a boy. When I found out I was having a girl, I was crushed! I knew my mother wouldn't be here much longer. I stopped going outside. I stayed by her side night and day, helplessly watching the effects AIDS had on her body! By this time, she lost her sense of smell, was always cold, and vomited blood a lot. It was so hard to watch. At the time, I became close with my female cousins who were sisters. Their mom knew I was labeled as trouble, but welcomed me to her home when I needed a mental break.

Not long after, I had the baby and gave her to my mother.

I had a dream on June 13, 2004 that I was at my biological mother's funeral! I couldn't tell anyone in my family. I told one person, and she said not to tell anyone else, so I didn't. I knew God was telling me that my biological mother was about to die. My biological mother came to me and told me a dream she had. She said, "Sherri, I had a dream of two tall angels who had on white robes. They were at the foot of my bed. One of them had a white robe in their hands for me!" I was speechless. My mom died August 5, 2004. At the end of the funeral, everything played out just like the dream. My nephew was born a month later. My biological mom never got to meet him.

I soon became so depressed. My boyfriend immediately started cheating and treated me terribly. He said, "You don't have anybody but me, so you need me!" I replied," If I have to live without my biological mother, I can live without you!" Deep inside, I felt that he was right. I gave my daughter up to one of my cousins. I went from weighing around 175 pounds to 129 pounds within months. I stopped eating. I wanted to die. I became suicidal. I would look at the closet in my room, and I thought about ways of hanging myself. Then I thought about my daughter and the pain she would feel.

For nine months, I went back and forth contemplating killing myself. Around 11:00 p.m., the thought would start. Then I would hear a knock at the door. My cousins would pop up. Night after night they came, and we just laughed. They didn't know I was suicidal, but God knew! He used them and my daughter to get me out of that depression. I got my daughter back. During this time, my family started becoming supportive. My godmother also apologized for any hurt she caused me, and of course, I forgave her. She's my mother.

I surrendered to the Lord, wholeheartedly. My mother's Section 8 went to me, so I was able to afford a townhouse. I was an adult now, so it was time to make some changes. I educated myself and others around me on HIV/AIDS. I made up my mind that this generational curse would end now. I took the limits off of what I could achieve and believed I could do all things through Christ who strengthened me. I became a great role model for my daughter because I knew she would learn from my actions; as parents, we are our children's first teachers. I dropped her father because he wasn't good to or for me. I was determined to never settle again in relationships, friendships, or life.

Before my mom passed, she would pray that God gave me a good husband. I started praying the same thing at this point. My cousin prayed for me one night, and God spoke that night. He said He has a husband for me who's a prince in His eyes, and he's going to treat me like a queen. He's going to give me the desires of my heart. He's going to love my child like he birthed her. We will have a big wedding, and we will bring a lot of souls to Christ.

I went home and wrote down every characteristic I wanted my husband to have, and I waited. While waiting, I prepared myself mentally, spiritually, and physically to become a wife. It was important for me to be in position, so I could be ready to receive the blessing God had for me. Two years later, God sent him. He worked where I lived. We talked on the phone for two months and then went on a date. While driving to the date, I realized this was going to be my husband! I was flabbergasted! We just clicked! He was everything I asked God for and more. The Lord gave me exactly what I wanted, even down to his facial features. I promise if you delight yourself in the Lord, He will give you the desires of your heart (Psalm 37:4).

We got married eight months later. My goddad was honored to walk me down the aisle. Before he passed he said to my husband, "Make sure you take care of my baby!" My husband gave him his word and he's a man of his word. I let Section 8 Housing go. Today, we have been happily married for fifteen years. We have four amazing children. We deal with each of our children differently, according to their personality, needs, and love language. God also gave me the gift of love for His children, so I started a childcare business. We are homeowners. We are active members of our church. This past summer, we graduated from the leadership academy. My husband is an ordained deacon and I'm an ordained minister.

Growing up, I went through a lot. I forgave myself and those who hurt me. I know that I had to go through this to help generations after me. I didn't understand the calling on my life growing up, and how the devil tried to attack my vision. I know now because I'm a prophetic seer. I can see in the physical and the spiritual. My life is not my own, but it's about pleasing the Father. Life is like a passing shadow, and depending on what you do while we're here will determine where you spend eternity.

* * *

My Word of Wisdom to You:

To the person reading this, while you still have a chance, please forgive so that the Lord can forgive you. I know you may be hurting, feeling discouraged, or maybe even feeling defeated, but don't give up! I came out on the other side victorious, and since you're reading this now, it's a sign that you will, too! Your testimony is on the other side of this test! You are valuable in God's sight! You can and will achieve everything God has for you! Don't give up! You've got this and God has you fully covered! To God be the glory!

You are a woman in pursuit.

I AM RESTORED

DAKIRIA JONES

Yup, it was just a regular day in the neighborhood! I was just minding my business, and this n*gga wanted to start early in the morning. I just wanted to have a good day, but I saw now it's going to be the opposite. He was knocking on the bedroom door like he just didn't put me and my kids out of the room he and I shared.

"How can I help you, Howard?" I said.
"Are you and the kids ready yet?" he responded.
"No. I need another 15 minutes. You can start the car," I replied.

I said to myself, "Just stay calm because I can feel like something is going to happen." About fifteen minutes later, I got in the car. Meanwhile, his phone kept ringing.

"Who's calling you?" I asked.
"Why?" he responded.
"So, now I can't ask you any questions?" I said.
"No, you can't," he replied.
In response, all I said was, "Okay, cool."

We dropped the kids off, and I headed to work. I was not making a big deal because I knew Tommy was going to be there, and he's the one I really wanted. I didn't know why I was still dealing with this clown. As soon as he picked me up from work, he wanted to argue. I wasn't going back and forth because I didn't even have the energy at this point.

I picked the kids up and dropped them off at their father's house. I had a party to go to that night, so that was the only thing on my mind, getting away from him. He came into the house and still wanted to fuss.

"Howard, I see your day is not going so well, so I'm going to just go in my room and chill," I said.

"You are not going anywhere" he screamed, as he pulled me by my hair.

I turned around and bit him on the face. He flipped me over and banged my head on the ground twice. Somehow, I managed to get him off me. He ran into my room, took my flower vase, and threw it at my head. I ducked. He grabbed another one and threw it at my mirror, shattering all the glass on my dresser.

The neighbor below us heard all the noise and called the police. The police arrived, but by that time, he had already left. I was asked a lot of questions and didn't provide any answers.

Hours passed, and he returned home. We didn't say anything to each other. I got dressed and left.

It was now 4:00 a.m., and my lover wouldn't stop calling. Yup, that's right, I wouldn't answer his calls. I entered the house, and he was still awake.

"Did you have fun?" he asked.
I said, "It was cool."

All I could think about was how I was going to leave this man alone before both of us died from domestic violence. My prayer was for God to remove this man from my life, and I knew sooner or later, He would. I said, "God, if you can remove him, I promise you I won't get back with him."

The very next day, he woke up and apologized to me for how he had been acting toward me. I accepted his apology, and we took a shower together. While in the shower, he told me he had something to tell me.

"It's okay, I already know," I said.
"So you know that I'm having sex with someone?" he said.
"Yes. The girl already told me," I said.

However, the truth was no one told me anything. I had a dream. God showed me who the girl was in my dream.

"So, you and Kim are having sex?" I said to him.

Kim and my sister were close friends. He went over to my sister's house from time to time to smoke. So, he was shocked that I found out. He looked at me like his heart had left his whole body.

"She told you?" he asked.
"Well, you didn't," I replied.

I got out of the shower, put my clothes on, and went to my sister's house because I knew Kim was there. I beat her in my sister's apartment and dragged her outside. She left her daughter in the house and ran. She found someone and used their phone to call the police, claiming that I had kidnapped her daughter. I took her car and left with the child still in the house. As soon as I left the apartment complex, the police arrived in a hurry. I was on the run for three days.

Eventually, I reached a point where I had had enough and decided to turn myself in.

While being locked up, I lost everything! My house, car, and three kids went to live with their biological dad, while Kim and Howard started a relationship. She thought she was taking my place, but little did she know, she was about to become another domestic violence victim in his book. The first few weeks, everything was perfect between them. And then suddenly, he changed. He got her pregnant, and she got him arrested for domestic violence. I heard all of this while I was incarcerated. All I could do was laugh.

While he thought I was hurting, God was healing me and opening doors for me. I couldn't see it, but He was working things out for me and my boys. My godmother said, "Daughter, you must go through the Father, the Son, and the Holy Ghost. Then God is going to open the windows of heaven and pour down all your blessings."

I heard everything she said, but I didn't have any faith. Six months is a long time to not see your family, hug your kids, pack their school lunch, take them to school, or kiss them. Those six months opened my eyes so much. All I could think about was the prayer I said to God: "God, please remove anyone in my life who is bringing me harm." And that's exactly what He did— quickly!

Domestic violence is a subject that does not need to be ignored. Most individuals do not know a lot of information about physical or mental abuse. While everyday reports about abuse have taken over the world and the lives of victims, many people are not aware of who is abused, the struggles that they face, and the humiliation associated with being abused.

While going through this entire process, I never questioned God. He had already shown me why! The strength I gained from being behind those walls was what I needed to move forward. Not only did God humble me for fourteen months, but He also showed me that even though He had taken everything away from me, for the next fourteen months, He would give me back everything I had lost.

"And I will restore to you the years that the locust hath eaten, the cankerworm, and the caterpillar, and the palmerworm, my great army which I sent among you."

I was blessed with a beautiful three-bedroom house for my three boys. I bought my first truck. All I could do was give God all the glory, honor, and praise. I felt so good again. I began to breathe again. I was able to see my boys happy again. I was nothing without God.

Now, four years later, I am happily married. My children are thriving in life. Life threw a few curveballs, but I am here today to tell you that even when you feel like life can't get any better, God has a blessing with your name on it. When it's your time, it's your time. Don't rush the process. Take it one day at a time, and watch God show up and show out in your life.

* * *

My Word of Wisdom to You:

Real transformation is only one thought away, whether it's good, bad, or otherwise! Believe in yourself to always move ahead for the better, no matter what! Always think greater! Love yourself enough to let go of false hope and grab onto real love.

You are a woman in pursuit.

I AM A SURVIVOR
TERRIONA WILLIAMS

O ne of the worst days of my life was August 29, 2020. My entire family was attacked by COVID-19. My brother, father, mother, and I had positive test results. We were so sick and the first to get knocked down. My brother and I had typical symptoms, including a loss of smell and taste. My dad had major headaches and sweat chills. My mom had body aches, a fever, and hurting bones. None of us knew what to do or even what this sickness was. This hit the world news! My mom endured thirty days of this sickness, as she seemed to not get up. Then later on, we all started feeling better. But then, out of nowhere, my health took another hit and gradually deteriorated. It was a COVID-19 nightmare in 2020. From the moment I learned I had COVID-19 until my hospital stay and capacity to recover, my experience with the condition was a nightmare.

It was a lovely morning. I woke up and started crying because I could barely get up and could not feel my legs. I remember it like it was yesterday. My eyes were bloodshot, swollen, and I was having trouble breathing. I also had a 105-degree fever. I immediately wondered, "Oh my God, is this COVID-19 again? Am I going to die?" I tried everything to delay the procedure, including taking a nap, taking medication, asking my mother to run me a bath with Epsom salts, and even stuffing an onion in my sock. Before going to the hospital, I did everything I could to treat my condition on my own and with my parents' assistance—but only until I could no longer bear it.

Then my parents rushed me to the hospital. Originally, we were heading for urgent care, but the pain was so unbearable, I could not take it, and it got worse by the second. I could not stand, so my parents carried me into the hospital until entrance security gave me a wheelchair. After that, a nurse arrived and started guiding me to the hospital's upper level where I had to ride the elevator and follow the doctor to the next available room. They had to put me on a stretcher and into an ambulance quickly after I entered the room in order to take me to another hospital. The nurses in the back assisting me were continuously monitoring my pulse, checking to see if my fever got worse, and even checking my heart rate all so quickly in fear of what would happen next. People were dying every day! My mind was racing and my thoughts were all over the place!

We were on our way to the next hospital. The medical staff hurried me back as soon as I got to the specified hospital. My thoughts were moving at a hundred miles per minute as many wires were connected to me. My heartbeat was getting faster every second. After that, they had to move me to another hospital. I had assumed that I had gotten over my COVID-19 nightmare, but little did I realize that it had returned along with a friend named MIS-C (multiple inflammatory syndromes), which tried to take my life. It was an inflammatory disease caused by COVID-19. My whole, entire body was inflamed with so much fire and heat, it had nowhere to escape. My eyes were bloodshot red, and my face was swollen. I couldn't swallow or eat as my throat was swollen, too. I needed assistance eating because my body was swollen, and my breathing was getting worse. I couldn't walk and was unable to move on my own. Never before had I experienced such excruciating pain; this was a nightmare, and I was in such agony that my head felt like it was on fire.

The doctor had to rush to give me medicine. It was immediately given to me to reduce the pain and swelling, and it put me to sleep. I was afraid to go to sleep. I tried my best to stay awake. I was *so* afraid I would not wake back up, but the medication they put in my IV sent me straight to sleep.

I awoke without knowing where I was since everything had become a blur. I had already lost a few family members at the time, but at that exact moment, I believed I would see them again. Boy, did I feel afraid! I was spoon-fed, carried to the bathroom, separated from my parents, and my bones grew weaker and weaker. Unbelievable! A COVID-19 nightmare! I felt like I was going to die in the next five minutes. I swear I was so scared.

We then found out my friend who I went to school with had died. She was fifteen years old– the same age as me. We went to the same school and now the same hospital. "God, what are you trying to tell me?" I was on the same floor she was! If I never believed in God before, I believed in him this time.

I was burning like I was in flames. The infection I had was trying to escape my body, but it had nowhere to go, and it became inflamed.

Lastly, during my recovery process, the doctors and nurses put me in isolation. I could not hold my mom or dad; all I had to hold on to was my faith in God. I kept thinking, "If I can just have one more chance at life, I will be the best me ever!" I became more grateful; it made me see life 100 percent differently, and I became way more appreciative. I said to myself after I recovered from this sticky situation, "I am going to chase my dream because life is not promised to anyone."

While in ICU, all I saw flash before me were my dreams and aspirations to finish school, and I heard my brother Terry's voice, who died, telling me loud and clear, "Terriona, stay in school, sis. Chase your dreams and become the best you possible!" I held on to that with everything in me and began to fight back COVID-19 like a bat out of h%ll and kicked MIS-C illness.

I remember my mom telling me, "Terriona, this is where your faith is tried and tested. This is one-on-one between you and God. Talk to God, and you pray." She lay her body on mine and began to anoint me and pray over my whole body in my room. She then said, "You are not going to die on my watch." Anybody who knows my mom knows she prays and prays and goes all out loudly. The doctors and nurses gave her peace once they saw her praying and looking through the door, waiting for her to finish.

The doctors told me I was going to stay there for one or two weeks! I asked God for two things: that was to please heal my body and let me come home with my family on my birthday. On the third day of being in the hospital, I said to myself, "Really!? I hope I won't be stuck in the hospital on my birthday!!" Well, a miracle took place the very next day. Six specialists came into my room after seeing all my vitals and said, "I don't know what happened between yesterday and today, but your daughter can go home today!"

I was like *what!* It was an *overnight miracle!* I was blown away! I remembered the words of my godmother, "Terriona, ask God for what you want." So, I did.

I prayed and asked God to please let me come home before my birthday! My faith in God and my mom and dad's prayers and all who were praying for me cracked heaven open! I was released *two days before* my birthday!

My recovery process was not as difficult as I thought. Once released from the ICU, my health began to get better. Now after my incident, I began to be more consciously aware. I was more sanitary and always kept my mask on. My appreciation for my doctors grew tremendously because of their professionalism and the continuous support I received once I left the ICU. Being in the ICU with patients sicker than me and succumbing to the illness was heartbreaking to me. My experience, my time in the hospital, down to my recovery process all reminded me that anything can happen at any time. My goodness, that was a nightmare. I just wanted to wake up and it all be over.

Today, I'm in college pursuing my dream of becoming a nurse to help people who have suffered like me. It was a close call! Thank you, God, for keeping your hands on me. Millions of people died during the COVID-19 pandemic, but I'm still here to tell my story. I'm so grateful. I'm moving forward to something greater and bigger. Although I faced obstacles since COVID-19, God still managed to keep His hands on me. I am 19 years old, and I feel it in my gut: the calling He has on my life is far greater than my imagination.

Every day, I spend an hour on self-care, reading my Bible, Sarah Jakes' book, journaling, and gaining motivation for the day! I currently work at Kennedy Krieger JHU Behavioral Health, where I find great pleasure in serving children facing daily challenges. I want to research behavioral analysis data. I come from a family of entrepreneurs, counselors, nurses, and doctors. My cousin, the first doctor in our family, was a huge motivation for me. We all grew up together, and they inspired me the most!

I'm here to tell my story: you can overcome anything if you put your mind to it and have faith! I've never seen a storm that lasts forever. Storms often come and go, but while you're in the storm, hold on. Never let go of God's hands until your change comes! Sunshine is right around the corner!

* * *

My Word of Wisdom to You:

Remember, you are an individual who finds strength to persevere and endure despite overwhelming obstacles. You gain strength, courage, and confidence from every experience in which you stop to look fear in the face. You can now say, "I lived through this horror!"

You are a woman in pursuit.

I Am Victorious

MARCIA WILLIAMS

I often ask myself many questions: Why did my body have to be a playground for Satan's workers? Why was I the target each time? Why didn't I understand all of his manipulations? Why didn't anyone notice the pain? There were so many questions running through my little mind. My body was not fully developed to match the weight of their huge bodies.

I had sandy brown hair and hazel brown/ green eyes. I was a little girl who loved ballet, modern, and jazz dance. I did not understand the role-play and the make-believe fake doctors examining my little naked body. I had no idea my first job was to take my clothes off and then be offered money as collateral to keep my mouth shut. I was just seven years old in second grade. What a powerful game that led me on a toxic journey! The playground became an amusement park, and the only difference was the same game, but different faces. *Why me?*

At the age of seven years old, a friend of the family molested me, forcing me to remove my clothes under threat. I was very young and felt confused and terrified. I did not know what to do. I was constantly told to keep quiet because no one would believe me. This continued for about three years.

At the age when the abuse began, I didn't even know how to start talking about my problems, emotions, pain, or trauma! I could barely even spell terms like *child molestation*, let alone explain it. I was a talented ballet dancer, excelling in my classes. I was the only black girl among many of my Caucasian classmates— the teacher's pet and favorite dancer. I consistently earned major roles in commercials, plays, concerts, talent shows, and dance competitions. You name it, and I was right there, front and center. I emerged as a leader in my own small way and was evolving into a smart, talented, and gifted girl at school until my innocence was taken away.

To cope with the pain and confusion, I would dance for healing, but eventually, the intensity of my emotions led me to drop out of dance classes. By the age of ten, I had become withdrawn, quiet, and shy at school. I couldn't bring myself to share my secrets with anyone because I felt too ashamed and frightened!

At the age of twelve, the same thing happened again— just a different face. I could not understand why I was targeted repeatedly. Despite my anger, I despised myself. I would take long showers and have crying spells throughout the night, hoping this would never happen again. Each time certain individuals were around, I would throw tantrums, make myself vomit, pretend to be sick, act out, or get in trouble for attention. School was my only comfort. I craved attention and care, but it seemed that no one could understand the signs and behaviors resulting from my traumatic experiences. I yearned for someone to lend an ear, offer a trusted comforting hug, and provide an outlet for help. Unfortunately, the caretakers in my life failed to notice the signs and understand my needs. I simply didn't know how to share it. I had convinced myself that no one would believe me. I was genuinely afraid to expose them, fearing shame and embarrassment. I believed I would be blamed and judged for something that wasn't my fault.

At the age of fourteen, I was raped by a fifty-two-year-old man. It felt as though I had become prey or numb after my initial experience of child molestation years prior. The trauma left me severely traumatized, mentally confused, emotionally disturbed, and devoid of self-esteem. I constantly worried that men could detect the scent on me or see the marks of pedophilic abuse on my forehead, attracting further violation into my life. As far back as I can recall, there were about three significant males who entered my family's life, each bringing their own share of mischief and trouble. Additionally, another male figure got dangerously close. He would frequently make inappropriate advances towards me, making crude verbal remarks about sexually assaulting me. I detested him. I tried to disclose the abuse to an adult, but my words were met with disbelief, despite my numerous attempts to verbalize that. So, I said, "What the h%ll." There was nothing I could do now. No one would believe me anyway!

My Life Out of Control

I began rebelling, running the streets, and engaging in heavy drug use with individuals who showed interest in me. I became highly promiscuous, dating older men and associating with drug dealers. Eventually, I found myself trapped in abusive relationships with men who unknowingly suffered from mental illnesses. I sank into a deep depression and felt utterly isolated in a world of my own.

Depression extends far beyond mere sadness or temporary difficulties; it is a grave condition that demands comprehension and intervention. This mental health disorder not only impacts the individual experiencing it but also affects their family, friends, and broader communities.

By the time I reached the age of fifteen, I was on my own. I spiraled downhill and dropped out of school; my life had become toxic and filled with stress. I resorted to smoking crack, snorting cocaine, and injecting heroin and cocaine simultaneously, a practice known as speedballing. During one incident, I experienced what can be described as a passing out, near-overdose, or what's referred to as O.D. on the streets.

My ex-boyfriend, who was also a user of intravenous drugs, injected an excessive amount of cocaine into my veins. Due to my fear of self-injecting, my ex-boyfriend would perform the injections on my behalf. The drugs overwhelmed my system, and I vividly recall the moment when my life seemed to flash before my eyes, as I slid down the wall. The quantity of drugs he had administered was more than I could manage. I recall sliding down the wall, hitting my head against the bathroom radiator, and losing consciousness. In that terrifying instant, I believed my life had ended. I was headed straight out! My life flashed before me!

As I slid down the wall, desperately clutching onto the radiator, I eventually collapsed onto the floor. Those who were present quickly applied ice-cold water to revive me and made me consume massive quantities of milk. Some left in fear of losing me. Miraculously, I regained consciousness, and it became evident that it was not my time to go, as God had other plans for me. Gradually, I returned to my senses. This experience frightened me to the core, and I decided that injecting drugs was a method I wanted to avoid. I knew then that there was a God! When I was in trouble, He cared and loved me enough to keep me alive.

"God is our refuge and strength, a very present help in trouble."

— PSALM 46:1

My God kept me!

I hated needles, but loved the feeling. Little did I know, it would later lead to consequences. No one educated me on heroin, cocaine, and other drugs that could destroy my life; all they said was to try it because it would make me feel good. As a result, I went through so much pain. Therefore, I was down for anything to take the pain away. I was desperate to escape life and reality; I felt like I was in a cold world all alone. Although distant, I felt connected to people whom I believed loved me. In my pursuit of acceptance, I ended up blending in with the crowd. Satan had it out for me! He knew what I would become later– a force to be reckoned with!

At that juncture, I had become completely disconnected from my family. I was too immersed in my destructive lifestyle to communicate and share my experiences. Consequently, I continued to smoke crack cocaine using a pipe. I resorted to using my body, once again, as a means to attain my desires. I engaged in manipulative games that I had been taught at a young age, to capture the attention of men and satisfy my addictive cravings. Consequently, my life began spiraling out of control. I initially ventured into the streets, nightclubs, and strip clubs, desperately searching for love in all the wrong environments.

Around the age of fifteen, I was no longer living at home. I was homeless. I resorted to constantly moving from one house to another and engaging in relationships with different men in exchange for a place to stay. Later, I got pregnant. Eventually, I made the difficult decision to undergo an abortion. At some point, I returned home briefly, but I eventually ran away again to escape back to the streets.

At sixteen, I found myself pregnant once again. This time, I wasn't willing to terminate another pregnancy. It happened quickly, again. She was the only thing I felt a pure, deep connection to— a connection filled with love. I didn't care if I was the talk of the city, or had nowhere to go with her, I was keeping my baby! Due to the love and connection that was flowing through my blood, I could not force myself to abort her!

While I was pregnant, I would sometimes sleep on the church steps for days. My daughter's paternal grandmother said to her son, "Get that girl and bring her to this house!" Once I was there, she fed me and offered me a nice shower. All I can remember is getting some really good sleep! I was dirty and hungry.

Soon afterward, I sought medical attention from an OB-GYN doctor, who helped deliver my 8 lb, 7 oz. healthy baby. Unbeknownst to me, he was an undercover pedophile. I was familiar with the signs, touches, looks, illness, and smell of a pedophile. Since childhood, God has given me a strong gift of discernment– a gift I didn't know existed, until later in life. Although I didn't know exactly what it was at the time, I knew something was off with my OBGYN doctor.

Pedophilia is a psychiatric disorder wherein an adult experiences sexual attraction to younger children. I was familiar with the actions of different men as they penetrated their fingers into my vagina. The same doctor who delivered my first child eventually took his life years later. This occurred after many investigations of finding out he was a pedophile, and the things he did to teenage girls in the hospital. He was caught and took his own life; he never sought the help he needed. This hit the world news. Once again, this highlighted the manifestation of mental illness at its worst.

At the age of eighteen, I became pregnant and underwent my second abortion. I was still in the streets and unstable. By the age of nineteen, I was pregnant again, and felt the same love connection. I gave birth to my second beautiful child. At twenty-two, I had my third abortion. At twenty-five, I delivered my third beautiful baby and felt that same love connection. All of these experiences involved different men. None of my daughters share the same father, but they were all my bundles of joy. My teenage life was like h%ll, but my three daughters gave me the most happiness and joy in the world! They were all I had and I felt real love. Two of my children's fathers remained absent from their lives. This trauma has haunted me throughout most of my entire young adult existence. *Why me?*

My oldest daughter's father is serving a life sentence in prison. The father of my second daughter is a recovering addict. The father of my third daughter was tragically murdered on the streets. The threat of Child Protective Services (CPS) taking away my children always loomed over me, but I continued to fight for survival. I was a fighting mother that was not going to give up! Freedom had to be around the corner— somehow and somewhere. I kept asking God: *"Why me?"*

My toxic, traumatized, and stressed state led me to become increasingly violent and hostile. I had reached a point of exhaustion and desperation, searching for direction and a way out, even if I appeared indifferent. All I yearned for was someone to recognize the pain in my heart and love me properly, in a healthy way.

After giving birth to my first two daughters, despite my struggles, I persisted in shooting drugs and smoking crack. There was no limit to the substances I embraced. During the delivery of my third baby, they believed she would be born a crack baby with an addiction. While I was pregnant, I was warned that she could potentially be taken away due to my crack use. So, I stopped using drugs while I was pregnant. However, by God's grace, she was born perfectly healthy. In 2 Corinthians 12: 9, the Bible says "My grace is sufficient for you, for my power is made perfect in weakness." God's Word became real to me. His hand continued to be over my life, despite the mistakes I made.

I found myself in and out of jail due to drug-related offenses. I was heavily immersed in the party scene, associating with high-profile drug dealers, traveling to acquire large quantities of drugs, and spending time with Jamaican boys who served as my suppliers and dealers. Eventually, my house turned into a crack house. People would gather to indulge in drug use, get high, and hide drugs in my house. I became a prostitute for money because that was familiar. That spirit of exchanging money for sex was already a familiar spirit.

Drugs, such as crack, heroin, and cocaine, were deeply ingrained in my lifestyle. I continued to snort coke and smoke crack, while simultaneously injecting a mixture of cocaine and heroin to find a sense of balance and numbness. My actions became a danger to myself. I grew weary and disenchanted with life itself, sinking into a profound depression and becoming exhausted with men and the cycle of domestic violence I endured. I felt trapped with no way out, and suicide consumed my thoughts. I resorted to taking pills and found myself admitted to a psychiatric hospital.

Once again, God saved my life! He kept stepping in. I just really wanted to be left alone to do me! Obviously, God had a purpose for my life that was *beautiful in His eyes!* I just didn't know when it would end. What's intriguing about my time at this psychiatric hospital is that little did I know, I would eventually find employment there later in my journey. I was blown away by God's goodness! God still saw me as worthy, in spite of myself and what others thought about me!

Such a lifestyle inevitably led to various issues, marked by a multitude of toxic problems associated with my chosen way of life. The abuse of psychoactive substances is classified as a drug-induced mental disorder, while the misuse of non-addictive substances is recognized as a behavioral disorder accompanied by physiological disturbances. Substance abuse is deemed harmful when the substance is consumed excessively, combined in a harmful manner with other substances, or used regularly without medical justification.

My experience of abuse began even though I was not aware of the dangers and harm it posed. Despite this knowledge, I continued down that path. My own house became a crack house, and it eventually became the target of a raid by law enforcement and other authorities. Everyone who ran other crack houses at the time were arrested. Their houses were raided and they were sent to jail, except me. *But God!*

The situation was both chaotic and peculiar because it appeared as though I was the one who had provided information about the drug dealers, which is commonly referred to as "snitching" in street terminology. I knew nothing and said nothing! But again, that was another God moment. Drugs were literally on my table, but I did not go to jail! As a result, I faced threats from drug dealers, and it became necessary for me to relocate and change my address. The police officers who were present in my house wore plain clothes, and posed as dealers. They saw something within me. One officer said, "Young lady, I don't know what it is about you, but please stop using drugs and take care of your children. You are too special for this lifestyle. God wants to use you." What he said brought me to tears. He was the first male angel and miracle sent to me by God! I felt like help was trying to find its way to me, as if God was saying that's enough!

I was totally confused, lost, and messed up by what the officer said. In all my life, no man had ever spoken to me with such care, compassion, or concern, unless he had ulterior motives, or wanted sex in return. Surprisingly, he didn't arrest me for the drugs found in my house, but he apprehended the drug dealers instead. They had been watching those drug dealers for years before the raid. On that same day, five other houses were raided, as well. Others went to jail, except me. I knew that it was nobody but God! God knew that I could not stomach Child Protective Services (CPS) taking my kids; they were all I had! They were my comfort and peace. I called all three of them my bundles of joy! Despite all that I went through and the toxic substances that affected my body, God's hand was truly on my life.

Psychoactive substances are substances that have an impact on the central nervous system. This interaction between substances and the individual is ongoing. While individuals make choices, it is the environment that influences and prompts those choices. The individual then responds to the consequences of their choices, and the environment reacts or adjusts accordingly.

Eventually, as ordered by the courts, I went into drug treatment, which turned out to be a pivotal moment that saved my entire life. During my time there, I had the opportunity to meet some remarkable professionals who recognized my potential and believed in my ability to achieve something meaningful. Each person played a role in nurturing my talents and imparting wisdom, as part of my drug treatment journey. I diligently followed their guidance, and was ready to rebuild my life. I underwent nine months of outpatient drug treatment, where I coincidentally met a man who was an ex-drug dealer and ex-drug user, who was also striving to turn his life around and recover from drug use. Today, he is my husband— Terry "Uncle T" Williams. He was the husband God sent to me! We are happily married and blessed with six children.

Terry embraced not only my present and future, but also my past with unconditional love. I knew he was the one for me. He cherished every aspect of me, from the hairs on my head to the very ground I walked on, and he was willing to do anything for me. It was a kind of love I had never experienced before. We crossed paths at a place called 911 JHH Drug Treatment Center, where he rescued me. We both were on a journey of overcoming addiction.

After completing the treatment program, I decided to return to my community and offer my services as a volunteer. The case managers and addiction counselors were sad to see me leave, and they even extended a job offer, which I declined. I chose instead to focus on furthering my education and continuing my journey of recovery and healing, addressing trauma at every level.

It was during this time that I encountered a very special person who had a profound impact on my life— my daughter's kindergarten teacher. She was a Caucasian woman, another angel sent by God to help shape my life. I couldn't fully comprehend why she chose to invest in me, but regardless, she motivated and supported me on my journey toward success. She never left my side. She led me to Christ! Sister Marty is an amazing evangelist and missionary. I accepted Jesus Christ as my Lord and Savior, and I began to build a relationship with Him.

I began attending church with Sister Marty, who introduced me to the amazing pastor of the church, Pastor Winnie Gilliam. Pastor Gilliam immediately took me under her wing, nurturing my gifts and talents. Her first words to me were, "Where have you been? You are my assignment," as if God had told her I was on my way, but had taken a long journey to reach her. I was a bit surprised and blushing when she asked where I had been because I had never met her before. In my mind, I wanted to say "to h%ll and back" because I had been through so much. However, I responded respectfully with a smile. Her glowing white and gray hair radiated a sense of peace to my soul. I knew I needed her in my life every day to guide me on this Christian journey called life. Later, she became a spiritual mother to me in every sense of the word, coaching me through life. I accepted Christ as my personal Lord and Savior. Then, my life took off like a rocket full of blessings. I started walking by faith and living my life according to the Word of God. I tried everything else. *Why not try Jesus?*

My life was becoming meaningful and beautiful! I had a reason to live and pursue everything God had for me, and more! Freedom was sneaking up on me.

My Metamorphosis

After giving my life to Christ, one of the first things He did was prosper me in my education and career. He allowed me to land my first job which was being an assistant school teacher. This brought me immense joy, especially when helping children facing life's challenges. I later changed careers and was fascinated by how the mind works in human behavior. I secured a position as a Mental Health Professional, working in a mental health facility in a clinical setting. I embraced clients who were just like me, and found my greatest passion serving them in every way possible!

While working in an organization as a Mental Health professional, I decided to continue my education. This employment opportunity deepened my fascination with the mind and various mental health disorders– including anxiety, bipolar disorder, PTSD (Post-Traumatic Stress Disorder), OCD (Obsessive-Compulsive Disorder), and drug addiction. Fueled by this passion, I aspired to return to school and study psychology, addiction disorders, and the underlying factors influencing human behavior and brain function. I graduated with a degree in Addiction Counseling and then pursued a Master's Degree to become a therapist, specializing in Licensed Clinical Professional Counseling (LCPC) within a clinical setting.

Additionally, I lead a private women's group named *Women in Pursuit*. Every three months, women come together with a shared objective: ensuring that no woman is left behind. Our motto is: "EmpowerED women empowER women." During these gatherings, we set goals and work diligently to achieve them. We aim to fulfill our desires and dreams, while striving to become the best versions of ourselves.

Furthermore, I hold the position of Assistant Director at an assisted living organization known as *Bundles of Joy*, a business founded by my daughter. The name for this organization originated when my three daughters were three, five, and nine years old, affectionately referred to as "my bundles of joy." Inspired by this term of endearment, my oldest daughter adopted it as the name for her business.

I also achieved a personal milestone by establishing my own coaching business called *Embrace Life Transformation*, which holds a special place in my heart. *Embrace* is all about teaching individuals to embrace everything that life throws at them. Instead of falling apart, we empower people with tools and skills to unpack their challenges one step at a time, ultimately moving towards greatness.

In addition to my coaching business, I also serve as the Vice Chair and Operations Manager for *Challenge 2 Change, Inc.*, a non-profit youth mentoring program. I find immense satisfaction in working alongside my husband, Terry "Uncle T" Williams, who is the visionary and CEO of *Challenge 2 Change, Inc.* I have developed skills in various areas, including: leadership development, team building, community collaboration, and the coordination of large projects aimed at strengthening families and communities. I am dedicated to helping women excel from pain to gain. I derive immense joy from motivating and guiding people to discover their purpose.

Currently, I'm working on establishing a transitional home called *Women of Transformation.* I want to help women who have been raped, sex-trafficked, incarcerated, abused, or are struggling with addiction or mental illness. Helping other women was also part of my healing process.

The Steps to My Healing

To heal from my traumatic experience, I took several important steps:

- *First*, I gave my life to Christ, recognizing that I couldn't overcome my struggles alone and needed divine guidance.

- *Second*, I had to forgive. I forgave myself and those who had harmed me. This emotional liberation granted me newfound strength and enabled me to progress in my life.

- *Third*, I joined a Bible-believing ministry that supported my spiritual growth and embraced Biblical truths. My faith in God played a pivotal role in my healing journey, propelling me to move forward. This can help increase your faith and allow God to reveal the beauty within you.

- *Fourth*, I joined a therapeutic support group. I surrounded myself with a supportive group of women who shared similar experiences. These women, whether married or single, were all pursuing dreams and goals while removing the weight of past hurts.

To heal, I had to step out of my comfort zone. I disregarded what others said about me and focused on making a positive impact on the world, particularly for women who– like me– had a voice, but were afraid to speak up. I shared my own hidden childhood challenges, which expanded my influence and allowed me to connect with others facing similar struggles. During my group therapy sessions, I recognized that I was also giving support to others, although I was there to receive support myself. My therapist recognized the gift of counsel in me. That's how my support group *Women in Pursuit* was started.

Women in Pursuit is a safe space for women's voices to be heard! Annually, we host a women's conference that celebrates our growth. We empower diverse groups of women who have experienced pain or trauma in their lives, whether highly educated or not.

However, before God allowed me to birth my support group, He first started with me! I was the first woman in pursuit! My journey is ongoing. I am no longer lost or stuck! I am pursuing and chasing purpose, as I continue to pursue my desires and dreams.

God cared about my growth and loved me unconditionally, despite my pain and mistakes. I never gave up on God. I maintained faith in God and myself, knowing that one day, my troubles would fade away– and they did!

My journey from being a victim, to becoming a victor, and ultimately a survivor was a remarkable transformation. I experienced beautiful moments of intentional spiritual breakthroughs, and education played a pivotal role in this process. It empowered me to access new opportunities, which I explore in greater detail in my upcoming memoir, *Why Me: From the Streets to the Pulpit*.

In my next book, I reveal how God transformed me from a life in the streets to a life in the pulpit. To God be the glory! So, stay tuned. There's more to come!

* * *

My Word of Wisdom to You:

Remember to keep moving because standing still is not an option. You were designed to grow, soar, and fulfill your purpose as eagles. Leave the past behind and embrace your journey with courage and determination.

Triumph lies in embracing the present moment and releasing the burdens of the past. By shifting your perception of yourself and awakening your inner strength, you have the power to transform your life. Your self-image determines your potential, and through personal growth and self-improvement, you can enhance that image. Don't let limiting beliefs hold you back or define your life.

Women in pursuit are those striving for something meaningful, be it a dream, a business, a relationship, a career, or any other goal. Ask yourself: "What am I in pursuit of?" Speak it into existence! I encourage every woman to relentlessly pursue what her heart desires. You have what it takes, and you deserve the very best.

You are a woman in pursuit.

WORDS OF ENCOURAGEMENT

To all of my 'Women In Pursuit' ladies
and the lives of women I've touched over the years:

Through God's grace
You mastered the pain
And called on His Name
You've kept the focus and aim
Even though you were drained
Your life was never in vain
To witness the spiritual rain
And how you've overcame
Without a doubt, you gained

Throughout the years
You were beautifully broken
But gracefully restored
You will never be the same
Continue to call on His Name

The *Gift!* The *Grace!* The *Power!*

To all the women who may be silently suffering:

Please know that there is hope and resilience within you. You are not alone, and the journey towards healing and transformation is entirely possible. Place your trust and belief in God's strength and His ability to help you overcome challenges, as stated in Jeremiah.

"For I know the plans I have for you, plans to prosper you and not to harm you."

— JEREMIAH 29:11

Allow God to be your guide. This begins with a commitment to trust. God cannot lead you where you will not follow.

"Trust in the Lord with all your heart, and do not lean on your own understanding. In all your ways acknowledge him, and he will make straight your paths."

— PROVERBS 3:5-6

Remember, don't give up on yourself. There is so much more potential inside of you. You may wonder, *"Why me?"* It's because you were chosen. Many are called, but only a few are chosen. You were built for this. You will overcome this. You've got it women!

TRIBUTES TO PASTOR MARCIA

"This mighty woman of God is phenomenal. She has helped to catapult me into my destiny. She is truly Heaven-sent! I thank God for this Queen's mighty valor and for being a prayer warrior. Her courage, strength to endure it all while standing, and her ability to still have a sound mind to survive— I know it was all God. For her to pursue her true purpose, she is truly a conqueror!

Pastor Marcia is truly favored by God. She is the Proverbs 31 woman: a mother to many, a dear wife, a loving sister, a dear friend, a phenomenal leader, and a woman of true character and integrity. Marcia is truly the real deal.

I am grateful that she never gave up and followed her call. I pray God continues to bless, push, and elevate her to maximize her fullest potential. For she stood the test time and time again. She is truly a blessing from God.

I love my mom and I'm beyond proud of the woman she has become. I would pick her over and over again to be my mother in any and every life. What a blessing. I thank God for her and I'm honored to be her firstborn.

— *Markia Cherry*

"I love Pastor Marcia and I am so proud of her! She has not only been my spiritual godmother, but she has been my mother, auntie, sister, and friend. Her passion for helping young women transcends anything I've ever seen. She knows us deeply, providing each of us with guidance, love, nurturing, and holding us accountable, according to what God allows her to see in us.

Pastor or Momma Marcia (what I like to call her) is relentless in her approach to ensuring we understand our assignment and the abundance God has provided us with. She doesn't allow us to just sit on our gifts and talents; there is empowerment in every word she speaks. For so many people I know, including myself, Pastor Marcia Williams is a beacon of light. We appreciate and honor the way she has walked in her assignment of being a vessel of God's enduring love and word."

— *Monique Debi*

M- Maker of Life
O- Outstanding
T- Teacher of Life
H- Healer of Pain
E- Extraordinary Super Woman
R- Reflection of God

"I've been tremendously blessed to have been raised and loved by the author herself. She has always been my guiding light at the end of every storm. Even when I wanted to give up, she would simply remind me that I was her daughter. And with that comes great trials and greater rewards. She knew I would be bent, pulled, pushed, and even broken! But She also knew God wouldn't allow me to give up! So, I just want her to know how grateful I am! I am thankful that she has given me life! I am thankful that she hears my silent cries! I am thankful that she hears my voice! I am thankful that she covers me! I am thankful that she pushes me! God knew that I needed a fighter and he blessed me with an incredible mom! She will always be the *hero* in my stories and my guiding light! I thank God for her and I love her dearly. She is my Mama Bear."

— Donique Lomax

"Pastor Marcia is an inspiration to so many women. She has been my spiritual guidance through my darkest days. She has been so much to us all: a leader, a mentor, a cheerleader, a superwoman. We all love and admire her."

— Ebony McClenny

"Throughout my 31 years of life, I've been blessed to be connected to an amazing woman. She has carried me through trials and tribulations— literally. She sees my strengths, weaknesses, successes, and failures. I want to always be able to pour back triple what she pours into me and others around me. I'm favored because of her.

She motivates me to keep striving, never stand still, stand apart, lead, and always leave something impactful on every person that comes into my life. She's a fighter. She's unstoppable. She deserves the world, plus more! She has left a mark on my life that could never be replaced, as well as on thousands of others, as well. I pray she experiences nothing but peace, blessings, abundance, and wealth. I love her and wouldn't ask for a better mother."

— Alicia Smith

"Pastor Marcia is a mother to the motherless. She will teach you, guide you, comfort you, correct you, celebrate you, motivate you, encourage you, uplift you, and most of all, she walks in love! She demonstrates all of the fruit of the spirit. She's a woman after God's heart. She sees the gifts in you and pushes you to birth them. I'm so blessed to have her in my life! I love you, Mama Marcia."

— Sherrita Coates

"I am thankful for Pastor Marcia. I thank God for her life. I am thankful for the wisdom, knowledge, and understanding she shares. I love the woman she is, inside and out. I appreciate everything she has taught me along the way. I appreciate the love she has given me. I appreciate everything she has done for me. Words can't express how grateful I am to have her in my life. I am thankful for everything God has in store for her life.

I'm blessed to have such a God-fearing woman in my life. She has blessed me in ways that can't be described. I am grateful to be a part of such a big project. I truly love this Woman of God."

— Dakiria Jones

"Pastor Marcia is my mother, a woman like no other. She gave me life, nurtured me, taught me, dressed me, fought for me, held me, shouted at me, kissed me, but most importantly, loved me unconditionally. There are not enough words I can say to describe just how important my mother is to me and what a powerful influence she continues to be. I love her with all of my heart."

— *Terriona Williams*

ACKNOWLEDGMENTS

I am so grateful for all of the love and support that I've received over the years from so many individuals.

To my amazing, phenomenal husband: Thank you for the push, support, and incredible love you show me every day of this journey! Thank you for the constant motivation and for building my prayer room, so I can have my private meditation, prayer, and writing time! Thank you for constantly drilling me about using my gifts and talents to make an impact and difference in the world! Thank you, bae!

To my mom: Thank you for teaching me how to overcome trials and tribulations as a woman! You have been my warrior and I've watched you endure many struggles. However, through it all, you've always remained on top! You are a praying mother, demonstrate tough love, and walk in complete wisdom and crazy faith!

To my dad: I will see you again one day. When you took your last breath, you said, "Go back to school. A big butt and a smile won't pay the bills!" Well, that degree that I was determined to receive is yours. All the others are mine!

To my children— Markia, Donique, Malik, Alicia, Marquise, and Terriona: Thank you for being mommy's bundles of joy! You have who beautifully overcame every obstacle and stood the test of time without breaking! In your words, as you always say: *"Won't he do it!!"*

To my brothers and sisters: Thank you for your diligence. No matter how life hits you, you've always managed to bounce back with so much power and strength!

To my godmother, Sister Marty: You are the most beautiful angel in the whole world! Thank you for introducing me to Jesus Christ and for teaching me how to have a beautiful, personal relationship with my Lord and Savior. You taught me great faith! And boy, do I have crazy faith! Nothing is impossible for God! You taught me that I can do all things through Christ who strengthens me (Philippians 4:13)!

To the late Pastor Winnie Gilliam: I will certainly see you again! All of the prophecies you've spoken have come true! You were my warrior.

To Bishop Brown: Thank you for speaking prophetically over my life and seeing things in me that I didn't see in myself. Your words "have you preached yet?" will always have an impact on me. All I could see was clouds and my head spinning, while rolling my eyes! Little did I know, I would eventually become a preacher!

To Bishop Bell: Thank you for your consistency. God assigned me to you. You spoke life to me in every season. You said, "I can't let you miss it! I gotta push you! Don't miss another season!" Those words completed and pushed the assignment God had for you for me. You pushed me right out of the nest, out of my comfort zone! Thank you for handling me with love and kindness!

To Mr. Achike Oranye: Thank you for showing me wisdom and grace on a professional level. Thank you for being my mentor and therapist. You've pushed and provoked me to excellence, and taught me not to accept anything less than excellence! You made it very hard for me, and you would not allow me to stop, quit, or give up!

About the Visionary Author

Marcia Williams serves as the CEO of *Women in Pursuit* and the Vice Chair/ Manager of Operations for the *Challenge 2 Change* non-profit youth mentoring program. She works tirelessly alongside her husband and children, deeply valuing community relation-ship building.

Education is important to her, as she holds a Psychology degree, Licensed Professional Counselor certification (specializing in Marriage & Family counseling), Child Development Associate (CDA), Addictions certification, and a Certified Transformation Life Coach.

Additionally, she is a Pastor of *Abundant Life Purpose Center*, mentor, coach, and motivational speaker– speaking at seminars, women's events, schools, churches, and conferences around the globe.

Marcia's non-profit coaching business called *Embrace Life Transformation* helps individuals get to the root of their behaviors.

Her greatest passion is pulling out the best in people! Her greatest joy comes from witnessing individuals excel, helping them become purpose-driven, and falling in love with the best version of themselves! Her motto is: *You got this!*

Printed in the USA
CPSIA information can be obtained
at www.ICGtesting.com
CBHW041144100424
6690CB00009B/528